The Storms Lifting

Written/Published by: Ms. Sue's

Dedicatng This Book To My Kids. I Would Not Have Made It
Through This Without Them

Table of Contents

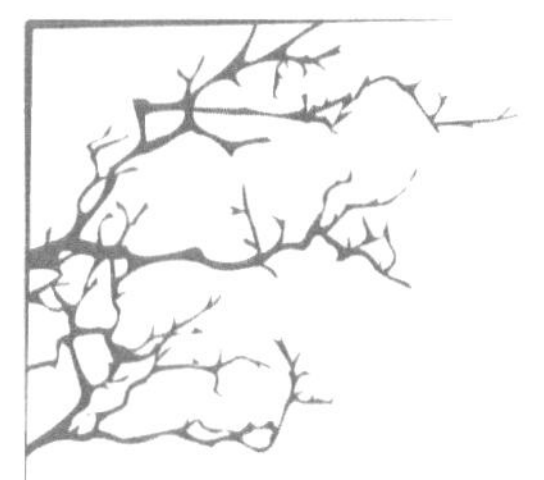

Prologue

Tulsa County had its own rhythm, a cadence that whispered through the tall grass fields and echoed off the red-brick facades of the small towns that dotted its landscape. To outsiders, it seemed like any other slice of Midwestern America—quiet, steady, unremarkable. But within the four walls of a certain suburban home, the Storm family's reality was anything but ordinary.

Lila Storm stood by the kitchen window, her hands trembling slightly as she wiped down the spotless countertop for the third time that morning. The early light of dawn filtered through the curtains, casting soft shadows across the room. To anyone watching, she was the picture of domesticity—a mother of three, dutifully tending to her home. But if they looked closer, they might notice the tightness around her eyes, the tension in her jaw, and the way she flinched at the sound of a car door slamming in the driveway.

Greg was home.

She heard the front door open, the heavy thud of his boots on the hardwood floor. Each step sent a shiver up her spine, but she forced herself to remain still, her breathing shallow, her movements precise. She knew what today would bring. She had seen it in his eyes the night before, that glint of something dark, something dangerous.

"Lila!" His voice boomed from the hallway, sharp and impatient.

She wiped her hands on the dish towel, folding it neatly before laying it on the counter. "In the kitchen," she called back, her voice even, controlled.

Greg entered the room like a storm front, his presence overwhelming, oppressive. He was a big man, broad-shouldered and thick-necked, with a perpetual scowl etched into his face. He scanned the room, his eyes narrowing as they landed on Lila.

"Where's breakfast?" he barked, as if the question itself was a challenge.

"On the table," she replied, nodding toward the spread she'd prepared—eggs, bacon, toast, all arranged just the way he liked it.

But he didn't move toward the table. Instead, he stepped closer to her, his gaze locking onto hers. Lila could smell the lingering scent of alcohol on his breath, could see the way his hands flexed at his sides, ready to strike.

"You think I didn't notice?" he said, his voice a low growl.

Lila's heart pounded in her chest. "Notice what?"

"Don't play dumb with me," he spat, grabbing her wrist with bruising force. "I know what you've been doing. Sneaking around, talking to people. You think I wouldn't find out?"

She winced at the pain, but kept her face neutral. "I don't know what you're talking about, Greg."

"Liar." His grip tightened, and for a moment, she thought he might strike her. But then, just as quickly, he released her, stepping back with a sneer. "You're not going anywhere, Lila. You belong to me. And you're going to remember that."

He turned and stormed out of the kitchen, leaving her standing there, her wrist throbbing, her mind racing.

Lila waited until she heard the front door slam shut, signaling his departure. Only then did she let out the breath she'd been holding, her shoulders sagging with relief. She knew the routine—Greg would be gone for hours, likely drinking himself into a stupor at some dive bar before stumbling home in the early afternoon. It gave her time, but not much.

She moved quickly, her steps light as she crossed the kitchen and slipped into the hallway. Opening a small closet, she pulled out an old shoebox, hidden beneath a stack of worn towels. Inside was the money she'd been squirreling away for months, dollar by dollar, every time Greg left the house. It wasn't much, but it was enough. Enough to get her and the kids out of here, far away from Greg and his twisted sense of ownership.

Lila took a deep breath, her mind resolute. This was the day. It had to be. She couldn't afford to wait any longer, not when she could see the darkness in Greg's eyes growing deeper by the day.

Her hands shook as she put the box back, closing the closet door with a soft click. She glanced down the hallway toward the bedrooms where her children still slept, unaware of the storm brewing just outside their doors.

"Not much longer," she whispered, more to herself than to them. "We'll be free soon."

But as she turned back toward the kitchen, she caught sight of her reflection in the hallway mirror. The woman staring back at her looked tired, worn, and scared. Yet beneath the fear, there was something else—a flicker of determination, a spark of defiance.

Lila straightened her spine, lifting her chin. Greg had tried to break her, to mold her into something pliable, something submissive. But he had underestimated the storm that was building inside her, a storm that would soon unleash with a fury he could never have imagined.

Today, she would take the first step toward freedom. And when the dust settled, Greg would find himself standing alone, cast out like the trash he had always treated her as.

Because Hell hath no fury like a woman scorned.

And Lila Storm was ready to unleash her wrath.

Lila tore her gaze from the mirror, feeling a surge of adrenaline course through her veins. There was no time to waste. She moved through the house with purpose, checking each of the children's rooms.

First, she stepped into Chloe's room. Her daughter was curled up under a thin quilt, her auburn hair spilling across the pillow like a cascade of autumn leaves. Chloe had grown up too fast, forced to mature in a house where fear was a constant companion. Lila gently brushed a strand of hair from Chloe's face, her heart aching with the weight of what she was about to do.

"Chloe," she whispered, giving her shoulder a gentle shake. "It's time."

Chloe's eyes fluttered open, confusion clouding them for only a moment before understanding settled in. She nodded, pushing the covers aside and slipping out of bed without a word. They had rehearsed this moment, and Chloe knew what needed to be done. Lila watched as she silently gathered a small duffel bag from the closet, already packed with essentials: a change of clothes, some toiletries, a few precious keepsakes.

Lila then moved to Lucas's room. Her youngest was still asleep, his small body sprawled across the bed in that careless way only children can manage. At ten, Lucas was still innocent, blissfully unaware of the full scope of his father's cruelty. Lila hesitated, not wanting to disturb his peace, but knowing she had no choice.

"Lucas," she murmured softly, sitting on the edge of his bed. "Wake up, honey."

Lucas stirred, blinking up at her with sleepy eyes. "Mom? Is it morning already?"

"Not yet, sweetheart. But we need to go on a little adventure, okay? Remember what we talked about?"

Lucas's brow furrowed as he tried to shake off the last remnants of sleep. Then, recognition dawned. "The secret adventure?"

Lila nodded, forcing a smile. "That's right. So let's be quiet and quick, okay? We have to leave before the sun comes up."

Lucas scrambled out of bed, excitement mingled with the confusion of waking up so early. He had always been the easiest of her children to calm, to soothe. It was Chloe who bore the brunt of the emotional toll, and Jaxon who internalized it, retreating into himself.

Speaking of Jaxon, Lila turned toward the room at the end of the hall. She paused outside the door, her hand hovering over the knob. Jaxon had grown distant over the past few years, his relationship with his father increasingly strained. He had once been a bright, hopeful boy, but Greg's harsh words and heavy hands had slowly chipped away at him. Now, at 21, Jaxon was a man in his own right, though still under the weight of his father's shadow.

She opened the door to find Jaxon already awake, sitting on the edge of his bed, fully dressed. His expression was hard, unreadable, but his eyes—his eyes were full of the same resolve that had kept Lila going all these years.

"Are you ready?" she asked, her voice barely above a whisper.

Jaxon nodded. "I've been ready for a long time, Mom."

Lila felt a lump form in her throat, but she swallowed it down. There would be time for tears later, time to mourn the years they had lost. For now, they needed to focus on the task at hand.

"Let's go," she said, turning back toward the hallway.

The four of them moved through the house like shadows, each one careful not to make a sound. They had practiced this escape many times in their minds, had whispered their plans in the dead of night, hoping and praying that Greg wouldn't overhear. Now, it was happening for real, and the gravity of the moment pressed down on Lila's chest, making it hard to breathe.

They slipped out the back door, the cool pre-dawn air hitting them like a splash of cold water. Lila took one last look at the house that had been both a home and a prison, its darkened windows staring back at her like hollow eyes. She had once dreamed of raising her family here, of filling these rooms with love and laughter. But those dreams had long since crumbled under the weight of Greg's tyranny.

"Mom, come on," Chloe urged, pulling at her arm.

Lila nodded, tearing her gaze away from the house. They hurried across the backyard, moving quickly but carefully, heading toward the car Lila had parked a few streets over the night before. She didn't dare park too close; Greg had eyes everywhere, or at least it felt that way. She had learned to be paranoid, to second-guess every decision, every move. But not tonight. Tonight, she would trust herself.

The car was an old sedan, nondescript and reliable. Lila had bought it with cash, under a friend's name, ensuring there would be no paper trail for Greg to follow. They piled in, Jaxon taking the front passenger seat while Chloe and Lucas settled in the back.

Lila started the engine, the sound too loud in the stillness of the early morning. She winced, glancing around to make sure they hadn't drawn any attention. But the neighborhood was silent, the houses dark, and she allowed herself a small sigh of relief.

As they pulled away from the curb, Lila felt the weight of years of oppression begin to lift, replaced by a nervous energy that kept her hands steady on the wheel. She didn't know what the future held, didn't know how they would survive on their own, but she knew one thing for certain: they were done living in fear.

She glanced at her children in the rearview mirror. Chloe was staring out the window, her expression a mix of hope and anxiety. Lucas had already dozed off again, his head resting against his sister's shoulder. And Jaxon... Jaxon was watching the road ahead, his jaw set in a hard line.

They drove in silence for a long time, the city of Tulsa fading into the distance as they headed toward the open road. The sun began to rise, casting the sky in hues of pink and orange, a new day dawning. It felt symbolic, a fresh start after years of darkness.

But Lila knew better than to let her guard down. Greg would wake up soon, and when he did, he would come after them. He wouldn't let go easily. He never had.

"We'll be safe," Lila said, more to herself than to anyone else. "We'll find a place where he can't reach us."

Jaxon nodded, his voice low and firm. "We'll keep moving if we have to. We won't let him find us."

Lila reached over and squeezed his hand, a silent thank you for his strength, for standing by her even when it wasn't easy.

They were far from safe, but they were together. And that was enough, for now.

As they crossed the county line, leaving Tulsa behind, Lila felt the first stirrings of hope. She didn't know where the road would take them, but she knew they were headed in the right direction—away from the past, toward a future that was theirs to shape.

And for the first time in a long time, she allowed herself to believe that they might just make it.

Chapter 1: After the Storm

The diner was nearly empty when Lila and her children walked in. It was one of those roadside places where the neon sign flickered, the booths were patched with duct tape, and the coffee was always a little burnt. But it was safe, and that was all that mattered.

Lila led her children to a corner booth, far from the windows. The waitress, an older woman with a tired smile, brought over menus and poured coffee for Lila without asking. She must have seen it all before—families on the run, people looking for a fresh start, or maybe just a place to catch their breath.

Lila wrapped her hands around the mug, feeling the warmth seep into her cold fingers. Her mind was still racing, replaying the events of the early morning over and over. She had done it. They were out. But the enormity of what came next weighed heavily on her.

Chloe slid into the booth beside her mother, while Jaxon took the seat across from them, with Lucas nestled against his side. The boy was still sleepy, rubbing his eyes as he tried to make sense of their new surroundings.

"Are we gonna live here now?" Lucas asked, his voice soft and a little confused.

Lila smiled, brushing a lock of hair from his forehead. "No, sweetie. We're just stopping here for breakfast. We'll be on the road again soon."

Lucas nodded, accepting the answer without question. It was one of the things Lila both loved and worried about when it came to her youngest—his ability to adapt, to trust that everything would be okay, even when it wasn't. She wanted to keep that innocence intact for as long as she could, but she knew the world was a cruel place, and they were about to face some harsh realities.

The waitress returned with a plate of pancakes for Lucas, a basket of toast, and eggs for the table. Lila hadn't ordered anything for herself. Her stomach was too knotted with anxiety to eat, but she watched as her children dug into their food, grateful that they had something warm and familiar in front of them.

"Jaxon, can you pass the syrup?" Chloe asked, her tone carefully casual.

Jaxon handed her the bottle without looking up from his plate. Lila noticed the tension in his shoulders, the way he kept his gaze fixed on the table. He hadn't said much since they left the house, and she knew he was struggling with more than just the physical act of leaving.

"Jaxon," she began softly, not wanting to push but needing to reach him. "How are you doing?"

He shrugged, finally meeting her eyes. "I'm fine, Mom. Just... tired, I guess."

Lila nodded, knowing there was more to it than that. Jaxon had always been the one who carried the weight of the family on his shoulders, even when he was too young to understand what that meant. He had tried to protect her, to shield Chloe and Lucas from the worst of Greg's anger, but it had taken a toll on him. Now that they were free, she wondered if he knew how to let go of that burden.

"We'll rest soon," she promised, reaching across the table to squeeze his hand. "We'll find a place to stay tonight and get some real sleep. I know it's been a long night."

Jaxon nodded, his expression softening just a little. "Yeah, okay. Thanks, Mom."

Chloe glanced between them, her fork pausing mid-air. "Where are we going to stay, Mom? Do you have a plan?"

Lila had thought about that question a lot over the past few weeks. She had a few ideas, but nothing was certain. They couldn't go back to Tulsa, not yet. Greg had too many connections there, and she knew he would turn over every stone to find them. She needed to buy time, to put as much distance between them and Greg as possible.

"I've been in touch with an old friend from college," Lila explained. "She lives in a small town a few hours away. I think she'll let us stay with her until we figure things out."

Chloe seemed relieved by the answer, nodding as she cut into her pancakes. "That sounds good. I just want us to be safe."

"We will be," Lila assured her. "I promise."

But even as she said the words, Lila knew that safety was a fleeting thing. Greg wasn't the kind of man to let go easily, and she had no doubt he would come looking for them. The thought of him finding them, of what he might do, sent a shiver down her spine. She pushed the fear aside, focusing on the task at hand—getting her children through the next few days, the next few weeks, without falling apart.

After breakfast, Lila paid the bill, leaving a generous tip for the waitress who had been kind enough not to ask too many questions. As they stepped outside, the sun was higher in the sky, the heat already beginning to rise. The day stretched ahead of them, full of uncertainty and promise in equal measure.

They climbed back into the car, and Lila pulled out onto the highway, heading west. The landscape began to change, the flat plains giving way to rolling hills and clusters of trees. It felt like they were leaving behind one world and entering another, one that held the possibility of a new beginning.

As they drove, Lila kept her eyes on the road, but her mind wandered to the future. She thought about the small town where her friend lived, a place where no one knew them, where they could start over. It wasn't much, but it was something. And for now, that was enough.

But as the miles ticked by, a gnawing worry began to grow in the pit of her stomach. She had done everything she could to prepare for this moment, but there were still so many unknowns. How would they survive on their own? How would she protect her children if Greg found them? And most pressing of all, how long could they keep running before they ran out of places to hide?

Lila glanced over at Jaxon, who was staring out the window, his expression distant. Chloe was dozing off in the backseat, her head resting on Lucas's shoulder. They were all exhausted, and Lila knew they couldn't keep this up forever. But she also knew that giving up was not an option.

"We'll be okay," she whispered to herself, gripping the steering wheel tighter. "We have to be."

The road stretched out before them, a ribbon of asphalt cutting through the Oklahoma landscape. The future was uncertain, but Lila was determined to face it head-on. They had escaped the storm, but now they had to weather the aftermath.

As they crossed into the next county, leaving Tulsa behind for good, Lila allowed herself a small moment of hope. They were free, at least for now. And as long as they had each other, they could face whatever came next.

But even as she tried to focus on the road ahead, a voice in the back of her mind whispered a warning: Greg wouldn't give up. He would find them eventually. And when he did, they would have to be ready for the fight of their lives.

THE SUN WAS HIGH IN the sky when Lila finally spotted the sign for the town she'd been searching for: Riverbend. It was a place she had only ever heard of in passing, but it represented a glimmer of hope, a chance to disappear into anonymity. Her friend, Kara, had moved there years ago after a bitter divorce, and in their few sporadic conversations, she had described Riverbend as quiet and welcoming—a place to heal.

Lila glanced at the clock on the dashboard. They'd been driving for hours, the tension in the car thickening with every passing mile. Jaxon hadn't spoken since they'd left the diner, his silence weighing heavily on Lila's heart. Chloe had drifted in and out of sleep, while Lucas, despite his earlier excitement, was beginning to show signs of the exhaustion that had seeped into all of them.

As they approached the town limits, Lila felt a mixture of relief and anxiety. Riverbend was small, the kind of town where everyone knew everyone else's business. That could be a blessing or a curse, depending on how well they could blend in.

"Mom, are we almost there?" Lucas's voice broke the silence, a thread of hopefulness in his tone.

"Almost, sweetie," Lila replied, forcing a smile as she reached over to squeeze his hand. "We're going to see a friend of mine. She has a nice house with lots of room for us to stay."

Jaxon shifted in his seat, finally turning his gaze away from the window. "You think she'll really help us, Mom? What if she tells someone?"

Lila heard the unspoken fear in his voice. He was right to be cautious—trust was a luxury they couldn't afford easily. But Kara had always been a loyal friend, someone who understood what it was like to live in fear. If anyone could be trusted with their secret, it was her.

"She won't," Lila said firmly, meeting Jaxon's eyes in the rearview mirror. "Kara's been through something similar. She knows what it's like to have to start over."

Jaxon nodded, though his expression remained guarded. It was a look Lila had grown accustomed to over the years—the look of someone who had been forced to grow up too fast. It broke her heart to see it on her son's face, but it also reminded her of how resilient he was, how strong they all had become.

They drove through the town, passing by a handful of small shops and a gas station. The streets were quiet, with only a few cars parked along the curbs and a couple of people out walking their dogs. Riverbend was nothing like Tulsa—there were no high-rises, no bustling streets. Just the gentle hum of a town that seemed to exist on its own terms, untouched by the chaos of the world outside.

Lila followed Kara's directions, turning down a tree-lined street until she spotted the modest, two-story house that matched the description. A wide porch stretched across the front, adorned with hanging baskets of flowers, and the yard was neatly kept, a few children's toys scattered across the grass.

"This is it," Lila said, pulling the car to a stop in front of the house. Her heart pounded in her chest as she turned off the engine, the silence that followed thick with anticipation.

"Are you sure about this, Mom?" Chloe asked, her voice small as she looked at the house with a mix of curiosity and trepidation.

Lila took a deep breath, trying to quell the doubts that had been creeping in since they'd left Tulsa. This was the best option they had, the only option that offered them a real chance at safety. "I'm sure, Chloe. Kara's a good person. She'll help us."

They all stepped out of the car, stretching their stiff limbs as they took in their surroundings. The neighborhood was peaceful, the kind of place where children played outside and neighbors waved to each other from across the street. It felt like a world away from the life they had left behind, a life where every moment was clouded by fear.

Lila walked up to the front door, her children close behind her. She hesitated for just a second before raising her hand to knock, the sound echoing in the stillness. There was a brief pause, then the sound of footsteps approaching from inside.

The door swung open to reveal a woman in her early forties, her dark hair pulled back into a ponytail, a warm smile on her face. Kara hadn't changed much since the last time Lila had seen her—a little older, maybe, with a few more lines around her eyes, but still the same person who had once been her confidante during those difficult college years.

"Lila," Kara said, her smile widening as she stepped forward to pull Lila into a hug. "You made it."

Lila returned the embrace, feeling a wave of emotion wash over her. For the first time in what felt like forever, she allowed herself to relax, just a little. "Thank you, Kara. For everything."

Kara pulled back, her gaze sweeping over Lila and the children. "Of course. I'm just glad you're all here, safe. Come on in, let's get you settled."

They followed Kara into the house, the cool air a welcome relief from the heat outside. The interior was cozy and inviting, with worn but comfortable furniture and walls lined with family photos. It was a home, in every sense of the word—a stark contrast to the place they had fled from.

Kara led them into the living room, where a large sectional couch took up most of the space. "You guys can put your bags down here for now. I've got a couple of rooms ready for you upstairs. It's not much, but it should be enough until you figure out your next steps."

Lila nodded, grateful beyond words. "This is perfect, Kara. Really. We're just so glad to be here."

Chloe and Lucas dropped their bags by the couch, looking around with wide eyes. Jaxon remained by the door, his hands shoved into his pockets, still wary despite the warmth of Kara's welcome.

"Jaxon," Kara said gently, addressing him directly. "You're a grown man now. I'm sure this hasn't been easy for you, but I want you to know that you're safe here. All of you are."

Jaxon met her gaze, and after a moment, he nodded, the tension in his shoulders easing just a fraction. "Thanks. I appreciate it."

Kara smiled, then turned back to Lila. "You must be exhausted. Why don't you all rest for a while? We can talk more later, figure out what you need."

Lila hesitated, feeling the pull of exhaustion but also the need to stay vigilant. "I don't want to impose..."

"Lila," Kara interrupted, her tone firm but kind. "You're not imposing. You're family, and family takes care of each other. Go rest. I'll keep an eye on things."

Lila felt tears prick at the corners of her eyes, overwhelmed by the kindness she had almost forgotten existed. "Thank you," she whispered, her voice thick with emotion.

Kara nodded, giving her hand a reassuring squeeze. "Anytime."

They made their way upstairs, where Kara showed them to two small but comfortable rooms. One for Lila and Chloe, the other for Jaxon and Lucas. The beds were made with fresh linens, and the windows let in a soft light that made the rooms feel warm and inviting.

Chloe sat on the edge of the bed, looking around the room with a mix of relief and uncertainty. "Mom, do you think we'll be okay here? Really okay?"

Lila sat beside her, wrapping an arm around her daughter's shoulders. "I do, Chloe. I think this is the place where we can start over. It won't be easy, but we'll figure it out together."

Chloe leaned into her mother's embrace, the tension finally leaving her body as she allowed herself to believe that they might really be safe here. "I hope you're right, Mom."

"I am," Lila said, though she knew their journey was far from over. There were still too many questions, too many uncertainties. But for the first time in a long time, she felt a flicker of hope.

In the next room, Jaxon helped Lucas get settled into bed, tucking the blanket around him like he used to when they were younger. Lucas yawned, his eyelids drooping as he looked up at his brother.

"Are we gonna stay here for a long time, Jaxon?" he asked sleepily.

Jaxon hesitated, unsure of what the future held but determined to protect his brother at all costs. "We'll stay as long as we can, Lucas. I promise."

Lucas nodded, his trust in Jaxon unwavering. "Okay. Goodnight, Jaxon."

"Goodnight, buddy," Jaxon whispered, watching as Lucas's eyes closed and his breathing evened out. He stood there for a moment, watching his brother sleep, before finally turning off the light and slipping out of the room.

Lila was waiting for him in the hallway, her eyes filled with concern. "You okay?"

Jaxon shrugged, though his expression softened as he looked at his mother. "I don't know, Mom. I want to believe that we're safe here, but I just... I keep thinking about what happens when he finds out we're gone."

Lila reached out, placing a hand on his arm. "We'll deal with that when the time comes. For now, we need to rest, to get our strength back. We can't live our lives always looking over our shoulders, Jaxon. We deserve better than that."

Jaxon

Jaxon nodded, though the worry in his eyes didn't fully fade. He had inherited his father's stubbornness but without the cruelty. Instead, he channeled it into protecting his family, something Lila both admired and feared. She didn't want him to bear the weight of their situation alone, but she knew how deeply he felt the responsibility.

"Go on, get some rest," Lila urged, giving his arm a gentle squeeze. "We'll talk more in the morning, once we've all had a chance to sleep."

Jaxon hesitated for a moment, then leaned down to kiss her cheek. "Goodnight, Mom. Try to sleep too, okay?"

"I will," Lila promised, watching him head back to his room. She stood there for a moment longer, the quiet of the house wrapping around her like a comforting blanket. The fear that had been her constant companion for so long was still there, lurking at the edges of her mind, but it was dulled by the exhaustion that pulled at her.

Finally, she returned to her own room. Chloe was already in bed, her breathing slow and steady, a stark contrast to the tension she usually carried. Lila brushed a hand over her daughter's hair, grateful for this moment of peace, however temporary it might be.

She changed into a pair of soft pajamas that Kara had laid out for her, then slipped under the covers beside Chloe. The bed was firm but comfortable, and as she settled in, Lila felt her body start to relax for the first time in what seemed like forever.

But as soon as she closed her eyes, the memories came rushing back—the years of fear, the nights spent listening for the sound of Greg's footsteps, the countless times she had told herself that she had to stay for the kids, that she couldn't leave. And then, the night they finally did.

She could still see the rage in Greg's eyes as she told him it was over, that she was taking the kids and leaving. The memory made her stomach churn, the terror of that moment still fresh. But she forced herself to focus on the fact that they were here, safe for now. Greg couldn't reach them, not tonight.

Lila rolled over onto her side, pulling the covers up to her chin. She had to stay strong, for the kids and for herself. Tomorrow would bring its own challenges, but she couldn't worry about that now. Right now, all she could do was take things one step at a time.

As she drifted off to sleep, Lila found herself thinking about the future. They were free from Greg, but that didn't mean their problems were over. There was still so much to figure out—where they would live, how she would support the family, what they would do if Greg ever found them. But for tonight, those worries could wait. For the first time in a long time, they had a chance to start over.

And Lila vowed to herself that no matter what, she would make the most of that chance. She would build a new life for her children, a life where they could finally be happy, free from the shadows that had haunted them for so long. It wouldn't be easy, but she was ready to fight for it. After all, they had already survived the worst.

As sleep finally claimed her, Lila dreamed of a future where they were all safe, where the fear that had gripped their lives was just a distant memory. It was a fragile hope, but it was enough to get her through the night.

And in the morning, they would begin again.

Chapter 2: Shadows of the Past

The morning sunlight filtered through the curtains, casting a warm, golden glow over the room. Lila stirred, her body aching from the tension she had been carrying for so long. For a moment, she lay there, trying to remember where she was, the events of the past few days blurring together in her mind.

Then it all came rushing back—their escape, the long drive, arriving in Riverbend. She turned her head to see Chloe still sleeping peacefully beside her, the covers pulled up to her chin. The sight brought Lila a small measure of comfort. At least for now, they were safe.

Lila carefully slid out of bed, not wanting to wake her daughter. The house was quiet, the only sound the distant hum of traffic on the highway. It was still early, but she knew she wouldn't be able to go back to sleep. Too much was running through her mind.

She dressed quickly and quietly, then slipped out of the room and headed downstairs. The kitchen was empty, but a fresh pot of coffee was brewing on the counter. Kara had always been an early riser, and the smell of coffee brought back memories of long conversations they'd had during their college years, back when their biggest worries had been exams and finding jobs after graduation.

Lila poured herself a cup of coffee and took a seat at the kitchen table, letting the warmth of the mug seep into her hands. She stared out the window, watching as the sun climbed higher in the sky, painting the town in soft morning light.

It was hard to believe that this quiet, peaceful place could be their new home. The idea felt almost foreign to her—home had always been a battleground, a place where she had to be constantly on guard. But here, in this small town where no one knew their story, there was a chance for something different.

The sound of footsteps on the stairs pulled Lila from her thoughts. She turned to see Kara coming into the kitchen, her hair still damp from a shower. She smiled when she saw Lila sitting there, though there was a hint of concern in her eyes.

"Morning," Kara said softly, crossing the room to grab her own cup of coffee. "You sleep okay?"

Lila nodded, though the truth was more complicated. "Better than I have in a while. It's just... hard to turn my brain off, you know?"

Kara sat down across from her, nodding in understanding. "I do. It's going to take time, Lila. But you're here now, and that's the first step. You don't have to do this alone."

The sincerity in Kara's voice was almost too much to bear. Lila had spent so many years isolated, cut off from the world by Greg's control. The idea that she didn't have to carry the burden alone anymore was both comforting and terrifying.

"I don't even know where to start," Lila admitted, her voice barely above a whisper. "Everything is so... uncertain. How do I keep my kids safe? How do I make sure he never finds us?"

Kara reached across the table, taking Lila's hand in hers. "You're stronger than you think, Lila. You've already done the hardest part—getting out. The rest, we'll figure out together. There are people who can help, resources for women in your situation. But for now, just take it one day at a time."

Lila nodded, feeling a lump rise in her throat. She had spent so long pretending to be strong, holding everything together for the sake of her children. But here, in the safety of Kara's kitchen, she allowed herself to be vulnerable, just for a moment.

"Thank you," she whispered, squeezing Kara's hand. "I don't know what I would have done without you."

Kara smiled, her eyes warm with understanding. "You would have found a way. But I'm glad you reached out. We've got a long road ahead, but you're not alone."

They sat in silence for a while, sipping their coffee as the morning light continued to fill the room. It was a rare moment of peace, and Lila tried to hold onto it, knowing that the challenges they faced were far from over.

The sound of footsteps on the stairs signaled the arrival of the children. Lucas was the first to appear, his hair a tousled mess and his eyes still heavy with sleep. Chloe followed close behind, rubbing her eyes as she stifled a yawn. Jaxon was last, his expression guarded but more relaxed than it had been the night before.

"Good morning," Lila greeted them, trying to infuse her voice with warmth despite the anxiety that still lingered beneath the surface. "How did everyone sleep?"

Lucas climbed onto a chair beside her, nodding sleepily. "Good, I think. Are we gonna stay here, Mom? With Aunt Kara?"

Lila glanced at Kara, who gave her a reassuring nod. "Yes, we're going to stay here for a while, Lucas. Aunt Kara has been kind enough to let us stay with her until we figure things out."

Lucas smiled, the uncertainty in his eyes fading just a little. "I like it here. It's quiet."

"It is," Lila agreed, brushing a hand through his messy hair. "And it's safe."

Chloe took a seat at the table, glancing around the kitchen. "What are we going to do today, Mom? Do we need to go anywhere?"

Lila hesitated, considering their options. They couldn't stay hidden away in Kara's house forever, but she wasn't ready to venture too far out into the world just yet. They needed time to adjust, to settle into this new reality.

"I was thinking we could take it easy today," Lila said finally. "Maybe explore the town a little, get to know the area. What do you think?"

Chloe nodded, her expression brightening. "That sounds good. I want to see what it's like here."

Jaxon remained silent, but Lila could tell he was listening, weighing the idea in his mind. He had always been cautious, and she knew it would take time for him to feel comfortable in this new environment.

Kara stood up, setting her empty mug in the sink. "I need to run a few errands this morning, but I can show you around town when I get back. There's not much to see, but I think you'll like it here. It's a good place to start fresh."

Lila smiled, grateful for Kara's support. "That sounds perfect. Thank you."

After breakfast, Kara headed out, leaving Lila and the kids to explore the house and get settled in. The rooms were small but cozy, filled with the kind of homey touches that Lila had always dreamed of having in her own home. There were framed photos on the walls, bookshelves filled with well-loved novels, and soft blankets draped over the furniture.

As Lila helped the kids unpack their few belongings, she felt a sense of normalcy starting to take root. It was fragile, like a delicate flower trying to bloom in the aftermath of a storm, but it was there. For the first time in a long time, she allowed herself to believe that they might actually be able to build a life here.

But even as she tried to focus on the present, the shadows of the past loomed large. Every creak of the house, every unfamiliar sound outside, sent a jolt of fear through her. She knew that Greg was out there, somewhere, and that he wouldn't stop looking for them. The thought was never far from her mind, a constant reminder that their safety was precarious at best.

After they had unpacked, Lila and the kids ventured outside to explore the backyard. It was a simple space, with a small garden and a few trees providing shade. Lucas immediately ran over to a tree swing, his face lighting up with excitement as he climbed on and started to swing back and forth.

"Be careful, Lucas!" Chloe called, watching him with a mixture of amusement and concern.

"I'm fine!" Lucas shouted back, his laughter filling the air. For a moment, he looked like any other eight-year-old, carefree and full of joy. It was a sight that made Lila's heart ache with both happiness and sorrow—happiness that he could still find joy in the midst of everything, and sorrow for all the times that joy had been stolen from him.

Jaxon stood off to the side, his hands in his pockets as he watched Lucas play. He was always the observer, the one who kept a close eye on everyone, making sure they were safe. Lila knew he was struggling to adjust to this new reality, but she also knew that he was strong enough to handle it.

As they watched Lucas on the swing, Lila decided to take a small step toward normalcy. "How about we go into town and grab some ice cream? I'm sure there's a place around here where we can get a treat."

Chloe's face lit up at the suggestion, and even Jaxon looked intrigued by the idea. "I'd like that," Chloe said, her tone eager.

Lucas jumped off the swing, running over to join them. "Ice cream? Yes! Let's go, Mom!"

Lila smiled, feeling a little of the weight lift from her shoulders. "Okay, let's go."

They walked into town, the streets quiet and the morning air fresh and clean. Riverbend was even smaller than Lila had imagined, with just a few blocks of shops and businesses lining the main street. But it had a charm to it, a simplicity that felt like a world away from the chaos they had left behind.

They found a small ice cream parlor at the corner of the main street, its front window decorated with colorful

IMAGES OF ICE CREAM cones and sundaes. The bell above the door jingled as they stepped inside, the cool air-conditioned breeze washing over them as they were greeted by the sweet scent of sugar and vanilla. The parlor was quaint and inviting, with a few booths along the walls and a glass display case showcasing a rainbow of ice cream flavors.

A young woman behind the counter smiled warmly at them. "Good morning! What can I get for you today?"

Lucas pressed his face against the glass, his eyes wide with excitement as he scanned the array of choices. "There's so many! I don't know what to pick!"

Chloe giggled, nudging him playfully. "You can't go wrong with anything, Lucas. Just pick your favorite."

Jaxon stood back, his gaze fixed on the menu above the counter. Lila could tell he was trying to play it cool, but she noticed the way his eyes lingered on the chocolate fudge sundae listed at the top.

"Why don't you each pick whatever you like?" Lila suggested, pulling out her wallet. "It's on me."

Lucas finally settled on a bright blue scoop of cotton candy ice cream, while Chloe opted for a classic strawberry cone. Jaxon, after some deliberation, chose the fudge sundae, though he gave a small shrug as if to downplay how much he really wanted it. Lila picked a scoop of butter pecan, her favorite since childhood.

They found a booth near the window, the kids eagerly digging into their treats. Lila watched them, a sense of peace slowly settling over her as she took a bite of her own ice cream. For a moment, it was easy to forget everything that had led them here. They were just a family, enjoying a simple pleasure in a quiet town.

As they ate, Lila noticed a few people passing by outside, some glancing curiously through the window at the newcomers. Riverbend was the kind of place where everyone knew everyone else, and their arrival would surely be noticed. She wondered what the townsfolk would think of them, but she pushed the thought aside. For now, it didn't matter.

The door chimed again as a man in his mid-thirties entered the parlor, his friendly demeanor immediately catching Lila's attention. He was tall, with sandy blond hair and an easy smile. His presence was commanding, yet unassuming, as if he belonged in this small town.

"Morning, Beth," he greeted the woman behind the counter, who smiled and waved.

"Morning, Sheriff. Just grabbing your usual?"

"Yep, can't start the day without it," he replied, nodding toward the coffee pot behind the counter.

As he waited, the sheriff glanced around the parlor, his gaze eventually landing on Lila and her children. His smile didn't falter, but his eyes held a flicker of curiosity.

"Don't think I've seen you folks around here before," he said, his tone friendly and welcoming. "Just passing through, or are you new to town?"

Lila hesitated for a moment, unsure of how much to reveal. She didn't want to draw unnecessary attention, but at the same time, she knew that being evasive might only raise more questions. Deciding on a balance, she offered a polite smile.

"We're new. Just got here yesterday, actually. I'm Lila, and these are my kids—Chloe, Jaxon, and Lucas."

The sheriff's smile widened, and he nodded in acknowledgment. "Well, welcome to Riverbend. I'm Sheriff Cole Bennett. If you need anything, don't hesitate to reach out. It's a small town, but we look out for each other here."

Lila nodded, appreciating his straightforward kindness. "Thank you, Sheriff. We're just getting settled in, but it's good to know there's a strong sense of community here."

He took his coffee from Beth with a nod of thanks, then turned back to Lila. "There sure is. And don't worry about fitting in—folks around here are friendly. I'm sure you'll feel at home in no time."

With that, Sheriff Bennett tipped his hat slightly and made his way to the door. Before leaving, he paused and looked back at Lila with a gentle, understanding expression. "If there's anything I can do to help, just say the word. Take care."

Lila watched him go, a mixture of relief and wariness settling in her chest. Sheriff Bennett seemed kind, but she couldn't shake the fear that came with letting anyone get too close. They couldn't afford to let their guard down, not yet.

Once the sheriff was gone, Chloe leaned across the table, her eyes wide with excitement. "He seemed nice, Mom. Do you think we'll see him again?"

Lila smiled, though it didn't quite reach her eyes. "Maybe. But for now, let's just focus on getting used to our new surroundings."

They finished their ice cream and spent the rest of the morning walking around town, familiarizing themselves with the local shops and landmarks. Lila made mental notes of the places they might need to visit—grocery stores, a pharmacy, a library. It was a small town, but it had everything they would need to start over.

As they walked, Lila found herself relaxing a little more with each step. Riverbend was quiet, peaceful, and there was something reassuring about the way life seemed to move at a slower pace here. The people they passed were friendly, offering smiles and nods as if they already belonged. For the first time in years, Lila felt like she could breathe.

By the time they returned to Kara's house, the sun was high in the sky, and the kids were beginning to tire. Lucas was the first to collapse onto the couch, stretching out with a contented sigh.

"This place is nice," he said, his voice sleepy. "I like it here."

Lila smiled, brushing a hand through his hair. "I'm glad, Lucas. I think we're going to be okay here."

Chloe and Jaxon settled in beside their brother, the three of them finally relaxing in a way Lila hadn't seen in a long time. She watched them, her heart swelling with a mixture of pride and relief. They had made it through so much, and now, they had a chance to start over. It wouldn't be easy, and there would be challenges ahead, but for the first time, Lila felt a glimmer of hope.

She headed into the kitchen to start lunch, the sound of the kids' soft chatter filling the house. As she prepared sandwiches, she couldn't help but think of Greg, the shadow of him still lingering at the back of her mind. But she pushed the thought aside. He wasn't here. He couldn't hurt them anymore.

For now, they were safe.

As she placed the sandwiches on the table, Lila took a deep breath, trying to hold onto the peace she felt in this moment. They had a long road ahead, but they would take it one step at a time. And with the support of Kara, Sheriff Bennett, and the small town of Riverbend, she was beginning to believe that they might just make it.

"Lunch is ready!" she called, and the kids came running, their faces lit with genuine smiles.

As they sat around the table, laughter and conversation filled the room—a sound that Lila hadn't heard in what felt like a lifetime. It was a small victory, but a victory nonetheless.

And as they ate, Lila allowed herself to imagine a future where this peace could last, where they could truly be happy and free. It was a fragile hope, but it was growing stronger with each passing day.

And no matter what the future held, Lila knew one thing for certain: she would do whatever it took to protect her children and give them the life they deserved. Here, in this small town that had already begun to feel like home, they had a chance to heal, to rebuild, and to finally leave the shadows of the past behind.

AFTER LUNCH, THE KIDS retreated to their rooms, eager to settle into their new space and take advantage of the quiet afternoon. Lila, needing a moment to herself, stepped out onto the small porch at the front of the house. The air was warm, with a slight breeze carrying the scent of fresh-cut grass and wildflowers from a nearby field.

She sat down on the porch swing, the gentle creak of the chains providing a soothing rhythm to her thoughts. The events of the past few days replayed in her mind, and she found herself grappling with the enormity of what she had done—what they had done. She had uprooted their entire lives, left behind everything familiar, and stepped into the unknown with nothing but the hope of a better future.

For so long, Lila had been trapped in a cycle of fear and control, with Greg's temper casting a shadow over every aspect of their lives. She had always known that leaving was the only way to protect her children, but the thought of what could happen if she failed had kept her paralyzed for years. But now, sitting on this porch in a small town miles away from the life they had escaped, Lila realized just how strong she had been to finally make the break.

The door creaked open, and Kara stepped outside, joining Lila on the porch. She held two glasses of iced tea, handing one to Lila as she took a seat beside her on the swing.

"Thought you could use this," Kara said, taking a sip from her glass. "You've had a lot on your plate these past few days."

Lila accepted the glass with a grateful smile. "Thank you. I feel like I haven't really had a chance to breathe since we left."

Kara nodded, her expression thoughtful. "That's understandable. You've been through a lot, Lila. It's going to take time to adjust, for all of you."

They sat in silence for a few minutes, the swing moving slowly back and forth as they sipped their tea. Lila found comfort in Kara's presence, in the easy companionship that had been missing from her life for so long.

"I keep thinking about how different things could have been," Lila said quietly, her gaze fixed on the horizon. "If I hadn't left when I did... I don't even want to imagine what might have happened."

Kara's hand found Lila's, giving it a reassuring squeeze. "But you did leave. And that's what matters. You're here now, and so are the kids. You made the right choice, even if it was the hardest thing you've ever done."

Lila nodded, though the guilt still gnawed at her. "I just worry about what comes next. I know we can't hide forever. What if he finds us? What if he…"

Kara cut her off gently, her voice firm but kind. "Lila, you can't live in fear of what ifs. Greg doesn't have control over you anymore. You've taken that power back, and you have every right to rebuild your life without looking over your shoulder. And remember, you're not alone. You have me, and now you have Sheriff Bennett and the people of Riverbend. We'll all do whatever we can to keep you and the kids safe."

Lila blinked back the tears that threatened to spill over. "I just want them to be happy. They've been through so much, and it breaks my heart to think about the scars they might carry because of it."

"They're resilient, just like their mother," Kara said, her tone reassuring. "They're already adjusting better than most kids would in this situation. And as long as they have you, they'll be okay."

Lila leaned back on the swing, letting Kara's words sink in. For so long, she had been fighting to survive, to protect her children from the nightmare they had been living in. But now, for the first time, she felt a glimmer of hope that they might actually have a future—a future where they could thrive, not just survive.

As the sun began to dip lower in the sky, casting long shadows across the yard, Lila made a silent vow to herself. She would do whatever it took to create a new life for her children, a life free from fear and filled with the love and security they deserved. She knew the road ahead wouldn't be easy, but she also knew that they had already overcome the worst of it.

Lila glanced at Kara, who was watching the sunset with a contented expression. "Thank you for everything, Kara. I don't know how I'll ever be able to repay you for all you've done."

Kara shook her head, her smile soft. "You don't owe me anything, Lila. We're family, and family takes care of each other. Besides, seeing you and the kids safe and starting over is all the thanks I need."

They sat in companionable silence as the last rays of sunlight faded from the sky, the day giving way to a peaceful twilight. The worries that had weighed so heavily on Lila's mind began to lift, replaced by a quiet determination. She had made it this far, and she wasn't going to let anything—or anyone—stand in the way of the new life she was building for her family.

When they finally went back inside, the house was filled with the cozy warmth of evening. The kids were in the living room, curled up on the couch watching a movie, their laughter a balm to Lila's soul. She watched them for a moment, her heart swelling with love and pride. They were stronger than she had ever given them credit for, and she knew they would be okay.

Lila joined them on the couch, wrapping her arms around Chloe and Lucas as they snuggled up against her. Jaxon sat nearby, his usual stoic expression softened by the contentment of the moment. Together, they watched the movie, the outside world fading away as they immersed themselves in the story on the screen.

As the credits rolled and the kids began to drift off to sleep, Lila felt a sense of peace settle over her. They had made it through the day, and tomorrow was a new beginning. For the first time in a long time, she allowed herself to believe that they were going to be okay.

And as she carried Lucas to bed and tucked him in, she whispered a silent promise to herself: no matter what challenges lay ahead, she would protect her children with everything she had. They were her world, and nothing—absolutely nothing—would ever change that.

As she turned off the light and closed the door to their room, Lila felt a calm resolve take hold. They had survived the storm, and now, it was time to rebuild. One day at a time, one step at a time, they would create a new life—a life where they could finally be free.

And as she lay down in her own bed that night, with Chloe nestled beside her, Lila knew that this was just the beginning. Their journey was far from over, but for the first time in years, she felt ready to face whatever came next.

Because she had already learned the hardest lesson: no matter how fierce the storm, there was always a way through. And on the other side, there was a chance for something new—something better.

With that thought, Lila closed her eyes and allowed herself to dream of the future, knowing that tomorrow was a new day, filled with possibilities. And whatever it held, she and her children would face it together, stronger than ever before.

Chapter 3: New Beginnings

The morning sun rose over Riverbend, casting a soft glow over the small town as it stirred to life. Lila awoke to the sound of birds chirping outside her window and the distant hum of a lawnmower, signaling the start of another day. The peacefulness of the town, so different from the chaos of their previous life, was a welcome change, and Lila was determined to embrace it fully.

She stretched and sat up, taking a moment to appreciate the stillness of the house. The kids were still asleep, their gentle breathing a reminder of the normalcy they were slowly beginning to find. Lila slipped out of bed, careful not to wake Chloe, and went downstairs to start breakfast.

The kitchen was bright and cheerful, with sunlight pouring in through the windows. Lila busied herself with preparing a simple breakfast—pancakes, bacon, and eggs. The familiar routine brought a sense of comfort, a small piece of normalcy that she clung to in the midst of their new life.

As she cooked, her thoughts turned to their plans for the day. Kara had mentioned a few local places that might be worth exploring, and Lila was eager to familiarize herself with Riverbend and its surroundings. She wanted to make sure they were settled in properly and to start building connections in the community.

By the time the smell of breakfast wafted up the stairs, the kids began to stir. Chloe was the first to emerge from her room, her hair tousled and her eyes still heavy with sleep.

"Good morning," Lila greeted her with a warm smile. "How did you sleep?"

Chloe yawned and stretched, rubbing her eyes. "Good morning, Mom. I slept okay. Is breakfast ready?"

"Almost," Lila replied, flipping the pancakes. "Why don't you set the table while I finish up here?"

Chloe nodded and headed to the dining room, her footsteps light on the wooden floor. Lucas and Jaxon soon followed, both of them yawning and looking slightly disheveled but excited at the prospect of breakfast.

The meal was a lively affair, with Lucas eagerly recounting his dreams from the night before and Chloe chatting about her plans for the day. Jaxon remained quieter than usual, his gaze drifting occasionally to the window as if he were still trying to process their new reality. Lila noticed, but she chose not to press him, knowing that adjusting to this new life would take time.

After breakfast, Lila and the kids got ready for their day out. They dressed casually, ready for whatever the day might bring. Lila put on a light jacket, though the morning was already warm, and made sure the kids had their small backpacks with a few essentials in them.

Kara arrived shortly after they finished getting ready, her car parked in the driveway. She greeted them with her usual cheerful demeanor, her eyes bright with excitement.

"Ready to see more of Riverbend?" Kara asked, her tone upbeat.

Lila nodded. "Definitely. We're eager to explore and get to know the town better."

Kara led the way to her car, and they all piled in, with Lucas and Chloe in the backseat, chattering excitedly. Jaxon sat in the front passenger seat beside Kara, looking out the window as they drove.

Their first stop was the local park, a charming green space with playground equipment, picnic areas, and walking trails. The park was bustling with activity—families enjoying the morning, kids playing, and joggers making their way along the paths. It was a far cry from the confined spaces they had been used to, and Lila could see the kids' faces light up as they took in the sights.

They spent the morning exploring the park, with Lucas and Chloe making friends with some of the local children and Jaxon wandering off to investigate the walking trails. Lila took a moment to relax on a bench, watching her children interact with their new surroundings. She felt a pang of relief seeing them so happy and engaged.

After a few hours at the park, Kara suggested they grab lunch at a nearby diner. The diner was a cozy establishment with a retro feel, its checkered floors and bright red booths creating a nostalgic atmosphere. They settled into a booth near the window, and Lila took a deep breath, feeling a sense of contentment wash over her.

The menu offered a variety of classic American diner fare, and they each ordered something different—hamburgers, fries, milkshakes, and sandwiches. As they waited for their food, Kara chatted with Lila about the town, sharing anecdotes and recommendations for places to visit.

"Have you had a chance to meet many people here?" Lila asked, her curiosity piqued.

Kara shook her head. "Not as many as I'd like. I've been busy with work and taking care of things around the house. But Riverbend is a friendly place, and I'm sure you'll find people welcoming."

Lila nodded. "I hope so. It's important for us to build connections here. I want the kids to feel like they belong."

Kara's eyes softened. "They will. And so will you. It just takes time. The more you get involved in the community, the more you'll feel at home."

Their food arrived, and they dug in with hearty appetites. The diner's food was comforting and delicious, and Lila enjoyed the simple pleasure of sharing a meal with her children and Kara. It felt like a small but significant step toward normalcy.

As they finished lunch, Kara suggested they take a walk around town to explore a few more shops and landmarks. Lila agreed, and they set off, enjoying the leisurely pace of the afternoon.

Riverbend was a small but charming town, with a mix of old-fashioned storefronts and modern conveniences. They passed by a bookstore, a local craft shop, and a quaint bakery with the most tempting display of pastries. Chloe's eyes widened with excitement at the sight of the bakery, and Lila made a mental note to visit it again soon.

They also stopped by the town's library, a stately building with large windows and a welcoming atmosphere. Lila was eager to get library cards for herself and the kids, knowing that it would be a valuable resource and a way to integrate into the community.

As they walked, Lila began to feel more at ease in Riverbend. The town's charm and the warmth of its people were beginning to ease her anxiety, and she felt a growing sense of hope. There was still a long way to go, but each small step felt like a victory.

By late afternoon, the kids were getting tired, and Kara suggested they head back to the house. Lila agreed, and they made their way home, the sun beginning to set behind them.

Back at Kara's house, Lila and the kids settled in for a quiet evening. The house was filled with a sense of calm, and Lila took the opportunity to spend some time with her children, reading them a bedtime story and tucking them in.

As she sat by Chloe's bedside, Lila felt a deep sense of gratitude. Despite the challenges they had faced, they were beginning to find their footing in this new place. The road ahead would undoubtedly have its obstacles, but for now, Lila allowed herself to savor the moment of peace and contentment.

When she finally turned off the lights and closed the door to the kids' room, she found Kara in the living room, curled up with a book.

"Thank you for today," Lila said softly, taking a seat beside Kara. "It really helped. The kids seemed so happy."

Kara looked up with a warm smile. "I'm glad. It's important for them to see that things are getting better. And it's important for you too."

Lila nodded, her heart full. "I know. It's just hard sometimes, trying to balance everything and make sure they're okay."

"You're doing great," Kara reassured her. "One day at a time, right?"

Lila smiled, feeling the weight of the past few days lifting just a little. "One day at a time."

As the evening wore on and the house grew quiet, Lila felt a renewed sense of determination. They were taking steps toward building a new life, and while the journey was far from over, she felt confident that they were moving in the right direction.

With a final goodnight to Kara, Lila headed to bed, ready to face whatever the new day might bring. She knew that their journey was just beginning, but for the first time in a long while, she felt hopeful about the future. And that, in itself, was a victory.

THE FOLLOWING MORNING brought with it the promise of new opportunities. Lila woke early, her mind already buzzing with plans for the day. After a quick breakfast of coffee and toast, she decided to take the initiative to make the house feel even more like home. She'd spent the last few days unpacking, but today she wanted to tackle a few more personal touches to make the space truly theirs.

As she moved about the house, she decided to call a local handyman she'd been referred to by Kara. There were a few minor repairs needed—a leaky faucet in the kitchen, a door that didn't quite close properly, and a loose cabinet handle. She figured it would be best to address these issues sooner rather than later, ensuring their new home was as comfortable as possible.

With her to-do list in hand, Lila picked up the phone and made the call. The handyman, a friendly man named Tom who had lived in Riverbend all his life, promised to come by later in the day to assess the repairs.

Once the call was made, Lila focused on making the most of the morning with the kids. She decided they would visit the local farmer's market, which Kara had mentioned was a great place to find fresh produce and locally made goods. The market was held on the town square every Saturday, and it seemed like the perfect outing for a sunny Saturday morning.

The kids were excited about the trip. Lucas, always eager to explore new places, was particularly enthusiastic. Chloe had already made a list of things she hoped to find, and Jaxon, despite his usual reserve, was looking forward to sampling some local treats.

They set out mid-morning, the sun shining brightly as they made their way to the town square. The market was bustling with activity, its stalls lined with colorful fruits and vegetables, homemade baked goods, and handcrafted items. The air was filled with the enticing aroma of fresh bread, herbs, and flowers.

Lila felt a sense of optimism as they walked through the market. It was lively and welcoming, with locals chatting and laughing as they went about their shopping. She was struck by how much more open and friendly the town felt compared to the anonymity of city life.

They spent the next few hours exploring the market. Lucas eagerly sampled apples and strawberries from various vendors, his eyes lighting up with each new taste. Chloe was fascinated by the handcrafted jewelry and homemade candles, while Jaxon enjoyed observing the various crafts and chatting with a local farmer about his produce.

Lila picked up a few essentials—fresh vegetables, fruits, and a loaf of homemade bread—and was pleasantly surprised by how affordable everything was. She also bought a small bouquet of wildflowers from a vendor who smiled warmly as she made her purchase.

As they walked back to the car, Lila couldn't help but notice how much more relaxed the kids seemed. They had been through a lot in the past few months, but moments like this, surrounded by the friendly atmosphere of Riverbend, seemed to help them settle into their new life.

Back at the house, Tom the handyman arrived just after lunch, his tool belt jangling with every step. He set to work on the repairs while Lila showed him the areas that needed attention. His easy demeanor and efficiency put her at ease, and she appreciated his straightforward approach.

As Tom worked, Lila took the opportunity to tidy up the yard, pulling weeds and trimming overgrown bushes. She found herself enjoying the physical activity, the sense of accomplishment that came with making the space look neat and cared for.

By mid-afternoon, Tom had completed the repairs, and Lila was pleased with the results. The leaky faucet was fixed, the door closed smoothly, and the cabinet handle was secure. She thanked Tom for his work and paid him for his services, grateful for the help.

With the house looking better and the repairs done, Lila decided it was time to take the kids out for a little adventure. She'd heard about a nearby nature reserve that was known for its scenic trails and beautiful views, and she thought it would be a great way to spend the rest of the afternoon.

The nature reserve was a short drive from town, and as they arrived, Lila was struck by the beauty of the area. The reserve was a mix of wooded paths, open fields, and a small pond. It was peaceful and serene, a perfect escape from the hustle and bustle of daily life.

They set out on a trail that meandered through the woods, the shade of the trees providing a welcome respite from the afternoon sun. The trail was relatively easy, with gentle slopes and clear markers guiding the way.

Lucas and Chloe took the lead, excitedly exploring the trail and pointing out interesting plants and rocks. Jaxon walked beside Lila, his usual quiet demeanor giving way to a thoughtful expression as he took in the natural surroundings.

As they reached a clearing with a view of the pond, Lila encouraged the kids to take a break. They sat on a grassy knoll, enjoying the tranquility of the setting. The pond was dotted with lily pads and surrounded by wildflowers, and the sound of chirping birds and the rustle of leaves created a soothing soundtrack.

They sat there for a while, simply enjoying the peacefulness. Lila watched her children, her heart full as she took in their happy faces. It was moments like these that made her feel hopeful about their new life.

As the sun began to dip lower in the sky, casting a warm golden light over the landscape, they started to make their way back to the car. The walk had been refreshing, and Lila felt a renewed sense of energy and optimism.

When they arrived back home, Lila was surprised to find a small basket of freshly baked cookies on the porch. A handwritten note was tucked into the basket, welcoming them to the neighborhood and offering help if they needed anything.

The note was signed by one of the neighbors, Mrs. Reynolds, who had lived in Riverbend for as long as anyone could remember. Lila was touched by the gesture and made a mental note to visit Mrs. Reynolds and thank her for the warm welcome.

As they settled in for the evening, the house felt more like home with each passing day. The repairs were complete, the yard was looking better, and the kids were settling into their new routine. Lila felt a sense of accomplishment and contentment as she prepared dinner, her heart lighter than it had been in a long time.

After dinner, they gathered in the living room for a family movie night, a tradition Lila hoped to continue. The kids chose a film, and they snuggled up on the couch, the warmth and coziness of the room a stark contrast to the uncertainty of their past.

As the movie played, Lila looked around at her children, her heart swelling with pride and love. They were adjusting, and while the journey was far from over, they were making progress. Each day was a step forward, and Lila was determined to make their new life as fulfilling and joyful as possible.

When the movie ended and the kids were tucked into bed, Lila sat down at the kitchen table, reflecting on the day. She felt a deep sense of gratitude for the support of her friend Kara, the kindness of the community, and the resilience of her children.

She took out a notebook and began to jot down her thoughts and plans for the future. She was determined to make the most of their new beginning, to create a life filled with happiness and stability. It wouldn't be easy, but she was ready to face whatever challenges lay ahead.

As she closed the notebook and turned off the light, Lila felt a renewed sense of hope. They had made it through the first few days in Riverbend, and the road ahead was filled with possibilities. She was ready to embrace the future, knowing that with each passing day, they were building a new and better life for themselves.

And with that thought, Lila went to bed, her heart full of hope and determination for the new beginnings that awaited them.

THE FOLLOWING WEEK was filled with small victories and adjustments as Lila and her children settled into their new life in Riverbend. Each day brought new routines and opportunities to connect with the community. Lila made it a point to visit local shops, attend community events, and introduce her family to their new neighbors. It was important to her that they felt a sense of belonging and established roots in their new environment.

One afternoon, Lila decided to visit the Riverbend Community Center. She'd heard that they offered a variety of programs and activities for all ages, and it seemed like a good way for the kids to get involved and make new friends. The center was a vibrant hub of activity, with classes and events happening in every corner.

As she walked through the doors, she was greeted by a friendly receptionist named Emily. Lila explained that she and her children had recently moved to town and were interested in learning more about the programs offered.

Emily smiled warmly and handed Lila a brochure. "We have a lot of great options for kids—art classes, sports leagues, and even a summer reading program. And for adults, there are fitness classes, workshops, and social events. Feel free to take a look and see what interests you."

Lila took the brochure and glanced through it. There was something for everyone, from art and music to sports and community service. She was particularly intrigued by the summer reading program for kids and the cooking classes for adults.

"I'll definitely look into these," Lila said. "Is there a way to sign up for the programs?"

"Absolutely," Emily replied. "You can sign up online or come back here to complete the registration. We're always happy to help with any questions you might have."

Lila thanked Emily and left the Community Center with a renewed sense of excitement. She was eager to get the kids involved and explore the opportunities that Riverbend had to offer.

That evening, after dinner, Lila sat down with Chloe, Lucas, and Jaxon to discuss the programs they might be interested in. Chloe's eyes lit up at the mention of the summer reading program, while Lucas was excited about the idea of joining a local soccer league. Jaxon seemed less enthusiastic but agreed to give the art classes a try, much to Chloe's delight.

The next morning, Lila went online to register the kids for their chosen programs. The process was straightforward, and she felt a sense of accomplishment as she completed the registrations. She was hopeful that these activities would help the kids integrate into the community and give them a sense of normalcy.

Later that week, Lila received a call from Mrs. Reynolds, the neighbor who had left the basket of cookies on their porch. Mrs. Reynolds invited Lila and the kids over for a coffee and chat, a gesture Lila was eager to accept.

On a sunny Friday morning, Lila and the kids walked over to Mrs. Reynolds' house. Mrs. Reynolds greeted them warmly at the door, her smile genuine and her eyes twinkling with kindness.

"Welcome, welcome!" Mrs. Reynolds said, ushering them inside. "I'm so glad you could come by. I've been looking forward to getting to know you better."

The interior of Mrs. Reynolds' home was cozy and inviting, filled with vintage charm and carefully chosen decor. She led them to the kitchen, where a pot of fresh coffee was brewing and a plate of homemade scones was waiting.

As they settled around the table, Mrs. Reynolds poured coffee for Lila and offered the kids juice. They chatted about their experiences so far, and Lila felt a sense of relief and gratitude for the warm reception.

"I wanted to check in and see how you're all adjusting," Mrs. Reynolds said, her tone genuinely concerned. "I know moving to a new place can be challenging."

Lila nodded, appreciating the sentiment. "We're adjusting well, thanks to the warm welcome we've received. The kids are excited about their new activities, and I'm slowly getting used to everything here."

Mrs. Reynolds smiled. "I'm so glad to hear that. Riverbend is a wonderful place, and we're lucky to have you as part of our community. If there's anything you need or if you have any questions about the area, don't hesitate to ask."

They spent the next hour chatting and enjoying the scones, with Mrs. Reynolds sharing stories about the town and offering helpful advice. The conversation was easy and pleasant, and Lila felt a growing sense of connection with her new neighbor.

As they prepared to leave, Mrs. Reynolds handed Lila a small bag of homemade cookies. "These are for the kids," she said with a smile. "Just a little something to welcome them properly."

Lila thanked Mrs. Reynolds for her kindness and promised to return the favor soon. She and the kids walked back home, the cookies a sweet reminder of the warmth and generosity they had encountered since moving to Riverbend.

The weekend brought more opportunities to explore. On Saturday, Lila took the kids to a local farmers' market event that featured live music, craft booths, and various food stalls. It was a lively affair, and the kids had a blast exploring the different stalls and sampling local treats.

Lucas found a stall selling homemade lemonade and was fascinated by the process of making it. Chloe was drawn to a booth with handmade jewelry and quickly picked out a bracelet that she loved. Jaxon spent some time watching a local artist paint and was inspired to try his hand at drawing when they got home.

As the week progressed, the kids started attending their new programs at the Community Center. Chloe joined the summer reading program and was thrilled with the books she received. Lucas began soccer practice and quickly made friends with some of the other kids on the team. Jaxon started his art classes, and while he was initially hesitant, he soon found himself enjoying the creative process.

Lila also began attending the cooking classes at the Community Center. She enjoyed learning new recipes and techniques and appreciated the chance to meet other local residents. The classes became a highlight of her week, and she looked forward to sharing her new culinary skills with her family.

As the days turned into weeks, Lila and her children continued to adjust and find their place in Riverbend. The initial challenges of moving and settling in gradually gave way to a sense of belonging and excitement about their new life.

One evening, as Lila sat on the porch with a cup of tea, she reflected on how far they had come. The road had been difficult, but each step they took brought them closer to the life they had hoped for. The house was becoming more like home, and the community was proving to be a supportive and welcoming place.

Lila looked out over the quiet street, feeling a deep sense of gratitude. The journey was far from over, but she was hopeful and determined to make the most of the new beginning they had found in Riverbend.

With a contented sigh, Lila finished her tea and went inside to join her children. They were gathered in the living room, their laughter and chatter filling the house with warmth. As she joined them, Lila felt a profound sense of peace and optimism for the future.

Their new life was taking shape, and for the first time in a long time, Lila felt truly at home.

Chapter 4: Adjustments

The days in Riverbend continued to unfold, bringing with them the rhythms of daily life and the gradual settling into new routines. Lila found herself becoming more comfortable with the pace of life in the small town. The kids were thriving in their new activities, and Lila was finding joy in her cooking classes and the growing connections she was making in the community.

One Wednesday afternoon, Lila decided it was time to tackle a project that had been on her mind since they moved in—the overgrown garden in the backyard. The garden had great potential, but it needed a lot of work. With summer in full swing, it was the perfect time to start transforming it into a space where they could all relax and enjoy.

She set out to the local hardware store to pick up supplies. The store, a small but well-stocked establishment with a friendly staff, was one of her favorite places to visit. She had already become a regular, and the employees greeted her by name.

As Lila perused the aisles, she ran into Mrs. Reynolds, who was picking up some gardening tools of her own.

"Hello, Lila!" Mrs. Reynolds called out, her face lighting up with a smile. "I see you're taking on a garden project. How's everything going?"

Lila smiled back. "Hi, Mrs. Reynolds. Yes, I'm planning to clean up the backyard and maybe start a small vegetable garden. It's been a bit of a task, but I'm looking forward to it."

Mrs. Reynolds nodded approvingly. "Gardening is a wonderful way to spend time. If you need any tips or advice, feel free to ask. I've been gardening for years and would be happy to help."

"Thank you, I might just take you up on that," Lila said, appreciating the offer.

After exchanging a few more pleasantries, Lila finished her shopping and headed home with bags of soil, seeds, and gardening tools. The kids were at a playdate with friends from their soccer and art classes, so Lila had a few uninterrupted hours to work in the garden.

The first step was clearing out the weeds and old plants. Lila worked diligently, her hands covered in dirt as she removed the overgrown vegetation. It was hard work, but she enjoyed the physical activity and the sense of accomplishment that came with it.

As the afternoon wore on, Lila took a break to catch her breath and admire her progress. The garden was starting to look more manageable, and she could envision the future it held. She decided to plant a mix of vegetables—tomatoes, cucumbers, and peppers—as well as some flowers to add color and beauty to the space.

When the kids returned home, they were excited to see the progress Lila had made. They joined her in the garden, eagerly helping to plant the seeds and water the newly prepared soil. Lucas was particularly enthusiastic, his face smeared with dirt as he dug small holes for the seeds. Chloe carefully placed the flower seeds in neat rows, while Jaxon watched intently, offering occasional suggestions.

The garden project turned into a family affair, and by the end of the day, the garden was looking much better. The kids were proud of their work, and Lila felt a deep sense of satisfaction. It was a small but significant step in making their new house feel like a true home.

That evening, as they sat down for dinner, Lila noticed how much more relaxed and happy the kids seemed. They talked excitedly about their day, their faces flushed with the satisfaction of their hard work. Lila felt a sense of pride as she listened to their stories, grateful for the positive changes in their lives.

After dinner, Lila took the opportunity to call Mrs. Reynolds and ask for some gardening advice. They had a pleasant chat, with Mrs. Reynolds offering helpful tips on maintaining the garden and dealing with common pests. Lila appreciated the guidance and felt more confident about her gardening efforts.

The following Saturday, Lila and the kids attended the Riverbend Summer Festival, a popular event that brought the community together for a day of fun and festivities. The festival featured live music, food vendors, craft booths, and activities for children. It was a great way to experience the local culture and meet more people in the town.

The festival grounds were lively and colorful, with families enjoying the various attractions. Lila and the kids wandered through the booths, sampling local food and admiring the handmade crafts. Chloe was particularly excited about a face painting booth, and Lucas was thrilled to find a stand selling homemade ice cream.

As they walked around, Lila bumped into a few of her new acquaintances from the Community Center. She was pleasantly surprised by how friendly and welcoming everyone was. It made her feel more connected to the community and reassured her that they were fitting in well.

Later in the afternoon, the kids participated in a few of the festival activities, including a sack race and a scavenger hunt. Lila cheered them on from the sidelines, her heart full of joy as she watched them have fun and interact with other children.

As the sun began to set, casting a warm golden light over the festival, Lila felt a deep sense of contentment. The past few weeks had been a whirlwind of changes and adjustments, but moments like these reminded her of the positive aspects of their new life.

By the time the festival drew to a close, the kids were tired but happy, their faces glowing with the excitement of the day. They headed home, carrying small prizes and souvenirs from the festival. Lila was grateful for the opportunity to experience such a vibrant and welcoming community event.

The next few weeks passed in a pleasant rhythm. The kids continued to enjoy their activities, and Lila's garden began to show signs of life. The vegetable plants were growing steadily, and the flowers were beginning to bloom. The garden had become a source of pride and relaxation for Lila, a space where she could unwind and connect with nature.

As August gave way to September, the transition into fall brought a new set of experiences. The weather became cooler, and the town started to prepare for the autumn season. Lila looked forward to the changing colors and the crisp air, eager to embrace the new season and the opportunities it would bring.

One evening, as the family sat together in the living room, Lila reflected on how far they had come. They had faced numerous challenges, but they had also found joy and connection in their new community. The house was becoming a home, and Riverbend was starting to feel like a place where they truly belonged.

Lila smiled as she looked around at her children, their faces illuminated by the soft glow of the lamp. The journey was ongoing, but with each passing day, they were building a new life filled with hope and possibility.

And as the days continued to unfold, Lila embraced the journey ahead, ready to face whatever came their way with resilience and optimism. The future was bright, and with each step forward, they were creating a life that was uniquely their own.

AS THE DAYS GREW SHORTER and the crisp autumn air settled over Riverbend, the Storm family adapted to the changing season with a sense of excitement and anticipation. The cooler temperatures brought with them the promise of fall festivals, harvest celebrations, and the cozy comforts of the approaching winter.

Lila was particularly eager to embrace the fall season, which brought with it opportunities for new experiences and traditions. She decided it was the perfect time to start planning for a Thanksgiving gathering. It had been years since she'd hosted a large family meal, and she was determined to make it a memorable occasion for her children.

One crisp Saturday morning, Lila and the kids ventured out to a local pumpkin patch. The patch, located just outside of town, was a popular spot during the fall season. It was a charming place, with rows of orange pumpkins scattered across a field, a corn maze, and various fall-themed activities.

The kids were thrilled as they wandered through the patch, searching for the perfect pumpkins. Lucas was especially excited, his eyes darting from pumpkin to pumpkin as he looked for the biggest one he could find. Chloe carefully selected a few small pumpkins, envisioning them as decorations for the house. Jaxon, who had initially been uninterested, ended up finding a pumpkin with an interesting shape that sparked his creativity.

As they made their way through the corn maze, Lila marveled at how much the kids had adjusted to their new life. They were laughing and enjoying themselves, their earlier apprehensions seeming like a distant memory. It was moments like these that reaffirmed her decision to move to Riverbend.

After picking their pumpkins and enjoying some hot cider and homemade donuts from a stand at the patch, they headed home with their bounty. Lila was eager to start decorating the house for fall, and the pumpkins would make a perfect addition to the seasonal decor.

Over the next few days, Lila spent time decorating the house with fall-themed items. She placed pumpkins on the front porch, hung autumn wreaths on the doors, and arranged a centerpiece of colorful leaves and candles on the dining table. The house took on a warm, inviting atmosphere that reflected the spirit of the season.

The kids were excited to see the changes and eagerly helped Lila with the decorations. They also started making plans for their Thanksgiving meal, discussing recipes and deciding on their favorite dishes. Lila was determined to make it a special occasion, and the kids were enthusiastic about contributing their own ideas and favorite recipes.

As the end of October approached, the community began gearing up for Halloween. Riverbend embraced the holiday with enthusiasm, and Lila was excited to experience it for the first time in their new town. She decided to take the kids to a local costume shop to pick out their costumes. The shop was filled with colorful and creative options, and the kids had a blast trying on different outfits and imagining themselves in their chosen roles.

Chloe chose a classic witch costume, complete with a black hat and a flowing cape. Lucas opted for a superhero outfit, excited to become his favorite character for the night. Jaxon decided on a more unique costume, a steampunk inventor, which reflected his interest in both creativity and mechanics.

On Halloween night, the Storm family joined the neighborhood trick-or-treating festivities. The streets were lined with festive decorations and houses adorned with spooky lights and cobwebs. The kids were thrilled as they walked from house to house, collecting candy and enjoying the festive atmosphere.

Lila took the opportunity to meet more of their neighbors and was pleasantly surprised by the warm welcome and friendliness she encountered. It was clear that Riverbend embraced the holiday with a sense of community and camaraderie.

As November rolled in, Lila began finalizing her plans for Thanksgiving. She decided to invite some of their new friends and neighbors to join them for the meal, hoping to create a sense of community and connection. She reached out to Mrs. Reynolds and a few other families she had met through the Community Center.

The preparations for Thanksgiving were a whirlwind of activity. Lila spent days planning the menu, shopping for ingredients, and preparing dishes. The kids helped with baking pies and setting the table, their excitement palpable as the day approached.

On Thanksgiving Day, the house was filled with the delicious aromas of roasting turkey, baking pies, and savory stuffing. Lila was pleased with how everything had come together, from the beautifully set dining table to the carefully prepared dishes. She was especially proud of the centerpiece she had created, a cornucopia overflowing with seasonal fruits and vegetables.

As the guests arrived, Lila welcomed them warmly, grateful for their presence and the opportunity to share the holiday with others. The gathering was filled with laughter, conversation, and the joy of good company. The kids eagerly showed off their costumes from Halloween and enjoyed playing with their new friends.

The meal was a success, with everyone enjoying the delicious food and sharing stories and laughter around the table. Lila felt a deep sense of fulfillment and contentment as she looked around at the happy faces of her family and friends. It was a moment of celebration and connection, a testament to the positive changes they had made in their new life.

As the evening drew to a close, Lila reflected on the journey they had taken since moving to Riverbend. The transition had not been without its challenges, but the experiences and connections they had made along the way were a testament to their resilience and determination.

The garden was thriving, the community had embraced them, and the house had become a home filled with warmth and love. Lila felt a renewed sense of hope and optimism for the future, confident that they were on the right path.

As she tucked the kids into bed that night, Lila felt a deep sense of gratitude for the life they were building together. The future was still unfolding, but with each day, they were creating a life filled with joy, connection, and the promise of new beginnings. Chapter 4: Adjustments (Continued)

As the days grew shorter and the crisp autumn air settled over Riverbend, the Storm family adapted to the changing season with a sense of excitement and anticipation. The cooler temperatures brought with them the promise of fall festivals, harvest celebrations, and the cozy comforts of the approaching winter.

Lila was particularly eager to embrace the fall season, which brought with it opportunities for new experiences and traditions. She decided it was the perfect time to start planning for a Thanksgiving gathering. It had been years since she'd hosted a large family meal, and she was determined to make it a memorable occasion for her children.

One crisp Saturday morning, Lila and the kids ventured out to a local pumpkin patch. The patch, located just outside of town, was a popular spot during the fall season. It was a charming place, with rows of orange pumpkins scattered across a field, a corn maze, and various fall-themed activities.

The kids were thrilled as they wandered through the patch, searching for the perfect pumpkins. Lucas was especially excited, his eyes darting from pumpkin to pumpkin as he looked for the biggest one he could find. Chloe carefully selected a few small pumpkins, envisioning them as decorations for the house. Jaxon, who had initially been uninterested, ended up finding a pumpkin with an interesting shape that sparked his creativity.

As they made their way through the corn maze, Lila marveled at how much the kids had adjusted to their new life. They were laughing and enjoying themselves, their earlier apprehensions seeming like a distant memory. It was moments like these that reaffirmed her decision to move to Riverbend.

After picking their pumpkins and enjoying some hot cider and homemade donuts from a stand at the patch, they headed home with their bounty. Lila was eager to start decorating the house for fall, and the pumpkins would make a perfect addition to the seasonal decor.

Over the next few days, Lila spent time decorating the house with fall-themed items. She placed pumpkins on the front porch, hung autumn wreaths on the doors, and arranged a centerpiece of colorful leaves and candles on the dining table. The house took on a warm, inviting atmosphere that reflected the spirit of the season.

The kids were excited to see the changes and eagerly helped Lila with the decorations. They also started making plans for their Thanksgiving meal, discussing recipes and deciding on their favorite dishes. Lila was determined to make it a special occasion, and the kids were enthusiastic about contributing their own ideas and favorite recipes.

As the end of October approached, the community began gearing up for Halloween. Riverbend embraced the holiday with enthusiasm, and Lila was excited to experience it for the first time in their new town. She decided to take the kids to a local costume shop to pick out their costumes. The shop was filled with colorful and creative options, and the kids had a blast trying on different outfits and imagining themselves in their chosen roles.

Chloe chose a classic witch costume, complete with a black hat and a flowing cape. Lucas opted for a superhero outfit, excited to become his favorite character for the night. Jaxon decided on a more unique costume, a steampunk inventor, which reflected his interest in both creativity and mechanics.

On Halloween night, the Storm family joined the neighborhood trick-or-treating festivities. The streets were lined with festive decorations and houses adorned with spooky lights and cobwebs. The kids were thrilled as they walked from house to house, collecting candy and enjoying the festive atmosphere.

Lila took the opportunity to meet more of their neighbors and was pleasantly surprised by the warm welcome and friendliness she encountered. It was clear that Riverbend embraced the holiday with a sense of community and camaraderie.

As November rolled in, Lila began finalizing her plans for Thanksgiving. She decided to invite some of their new friends and neighbors to join them for the meal, hoping to create a sense of community and connection. She reached out to Mrs. Reynolds and a few other families she had met through the Community Center.

The preparations for Thanksgiving were a whirlwind of activity. Lila spent days planning the menu, shopping for ingredients, and preparing dishes. The kids helped with baking pies and setting the table, their excitement palpable as the day approached.

On Thanksgiving Day, the house was filled with the delicious aromas of roasting turkey, baking pies, and savory stuffing. Lila was pleased with how everything had come together, from the beautifully set dining table to the carefully prepared dishes. She was especially proud of the centerpiece she had created, a cornucopia overflowing with seasonal fruits and vegetables.

As the guests arrived, Lila welcomed them warmly, grateful for their presence and the opportunity to share the holiday with others. The gathering was filled with laughter, conversation, and the joy of good company. The kids eagerly showed off their costumes from Halloween and enjoyed playing with their new friends.

The meal was a success, with everyone enjoying the delicious food and sharing stories and laughter around the table. Lila felt a deep sense of fulfillment and contentment as she looked around at the happy faces of her family and friends. It was a moment of celebration and connection, a testament to the positive changes they had made in their new life.

As the evening drew to a close, Lila reflected on the journey they had taken since moving to Riverbend. The transition had not been without its challenges, but the experiences and connections they had made along the way were a testament to their resilience and determination.

The garden was thriving, the community had embraced them, and the house had become a home filled with warmth and love. Lila felt a renewed sense of hope and optimism for the future, confident that they were on the right path.

As she tucked the kids into bed that night, Lila felt a deep sense of gratitude for the life they were building together. The future was still unfolding, but with each day, they were creating a life filled with joy, connection, and the promise of new beginnings. Chapter 4: Adjustments (Continued)

As the days grew shorter and the crisp autumn air settled over Riverbend, the Storm family adapted to the changing season with a sense of excitement and anticipation. The cooler temperatures brought with them the promise of fall festivals, harvest celebrations, and the cozy comforts of the approaching winter.

Lila was particularly eager to embrace the fall season, which brought with it opportunities for new experiences and traditions. She decided it was the perfect time to start planning for a Thanksgiving gathering. It had been years since she'd hosted a large family meal, and she was determined to make it a memorable occasion for her children.

One crisp Saturday morning, Lila and the kids ventured out to a local pumpkin patch. The patch, located just outside of town, was a popular spot during the fall season. It was a charming place, with rows of orange pumpkins scattered across a field, a corn maze, and various fall-themed activities.

The kids were thrilled as they wandered through the patch, searching for the perfect pumpkins. Lucas was especially excited, his eyes darting from pumpkin to pumpkin as he looked for the biggest one he could find. Chloe carefully selected a few small pumpkins, envisioning them as decorations for the house. Jaxon, who had initially been uninterested, ended up finding a pumpkin with an interesting shape that sparked his creativity.

As they made their way through the corn maze, Lila marveled at how much the kids had adjusted to their new life. They were laughing and enjoying themselves, their earlier apprehensions seeming like a distant memory. It was moments like these that reaffirmed her decision to move to Riverbend.

After picking their pumpkins and enjoying some hot cider and homemade donuts from a stand at the patch, they headed home with their bounty. Lila was eager to start decorating the house for fall, and the pumpkins would make a perfect addition to the seasonal decor.

Over the next few days, Lila spent time decorating the house with fall-themed items. She placed pumpkins on the front porch, hung autumn wreaths on the doors, and arranged a centerpiece of colorful leaves and candles on the dining table. The house took on a warm, inviting atmosphere that reflected the spirit of the season.

The kids were excited to see the changes and eagerly helped Lila with the decorations. They also started making plans for their Thanksgiving meal, discussing recipes and deciding on their favorite dishes. Lila was determined to make it a special occasion, and the kids were enthusiastic about contributing their own ideas and favorite recipes.

As the end of October approached, the community began gearing up for Halloween. Riverbend embraced the holiday with enthusiasm, and Lila was excited to experience it for the first time in their new town. She decided to take the kids to a local costume shop to pick out their costumes. The shop was filled with colorful and creative options, and the kids had a blast trying on different outfits and imagining themselves in their chosen roles.

Chloe chose a classic witch costume, complete with a black hat and a flowing cape. Lucas opted for a superhero outfit, excited to become his favorite character for the night. Jaxon decided on a more unique costume, a steampunk inventor, which reflected his interest in both creativity and mechanics.

On Halloween night, the Storm family joined the neighborhood trick-or-treating festivities. The streets were lined with festive decorations and houses adorned with spooky lights and cobwebs. The kids were thrilled as they walked from house to house, collecting candy and enjoying the festive atmosphere.

Lila took the opportunity to meet more of their neighbors and was pleasantly surprised by the warm welcome and friendliness she encountered. It was clear that Riverbend embraced the holiday with a sense of community and camaraderie.

As November rolled in, Lila began finalizing her plans for Thanksgiving. She decided to invite some of their new friends and neighbors to join them for the meal, hoping to create a sense of community and connection. She reached out to Mrs. Reynolds and a few other families she had met through the Community Center.

The preparations for Thanksgiving were a whirlwind of activity. Lila spent days planning the menu, shopping for ingredients, and preparing dishes. The kids helped with baking pies and setting the table, their excitement palpable as the day approached.

On Thanksgiving Day, the house was filled with the delicious aromas of roasting turkey, baking pies, and savory stuffing. Lila was pleased with how everything had come together, from the beautifully set dining table to the carefully prepared dishes. She was especially proud of the centerpiece she had created, a cornucopia overflowing with seasonal fruits and vegetables.

As the guests arrived, Lila welcomed them warmly, grateful for their presence and the opportunity to share the holiday with others. The gathering was filled with laughter, conversation, and the joy of good company. The kids eagerly showed off their costumes from Halloween and enjoyed playing with their new friends.

The meal was a success, with everyone enjoying the delicious food and sharing stories and laughter around the table. Lila felt a deep sense of fulfillment and contentment as she looked around at the happy faces of her family and friends. It was a moment of celebration and connection, a testament to the positive changes they had made in their new life.

As the evening drew to a close, Lila reflected on the journey they had taken since moving to Riverbend. The transition had not been without its challenges, but the experiences and connections they had made along the way were a testament to their resilience and determination.

The garden was thriving, the community had embraced them, and the house had become a home filled with warmth and love. Lila felt a renewed sense of hope and optimism for the future, confident that they were on the right path.

As she tucked the kids into bed that night, Lila felt a deep sense of gratitude for the life they were building together. The future was still unfolding, but with each day, they were creating a life filled with joy, connection, and the promise of new beginnings.

THE WINTER CHILL ARRIVED in Riverbend, bringing with it the first signs of snow. The small town transformed into a picturesque winter wonderland, with snowflakes gently falling and blanketing the streets and rooftops in white. The Storm family embraced the season with enthusiasm, finding new ways to enjoy their cozy surroundings.

One Saturday morning, Lila and the kids decided to make the most of the snowfall. They bundled up in warm clothes and ventured outside to build a snowman. The air was crisp and refreshing, and the kids were eager to get started. They rolled large snowballs, stacked them up, and carefully crafted a snowman with a carrot nose, coal eyes, and a scarf.

As they worked, Lila noticed how much more at ease the kids seemed. Their laughter and playful banter filled the crisp air, and Lila felt a sense of contentment as she watched them enjoy themselves. The snowman stood proudly in the front yard, a cheerful symbol of their new life in Riverbend.

Later that afternoon, Lila decided to bake some cookies to warm up from the cold. She invited the kids to help, and together they made a batch of gingerbread cookies, filling the house with the comforting aroma of cinnamon and spices. As they decorated the cookies with colorful icing and sprinkles, Chloe, Lucas, and Jaxon each expressed their creativity, turning the cookies into festive works of art.

The holiday season was in full swing, and Lila was determined to create new traditions for their family. She planned a holiday movie night, complete with hot cocoa and popcorn, and invited Mrs. Reynolds and a few other friends to join them. The living room was transformed into a cozy movie space, with blankets and pillows scattered on the floor and a stack of holiday-themed movies ready to go.

The night of the movie marathon arrived, and Lila and the kids were excited to share their new traditions with their friends. Mrs. Reynolds arrived with a tray of homemade cookies and joined in the festivities, bringing warmth and cheer to the gathering. The kids enjoyed watching the movies and playing with their friends, while Lila and the adults caught up and shared stories.

As the evening drew to a close, Lila felt a deep sense of satisfaction. The holiday season was turning out to be everything she had hoped for, and the connections they were making in Riverbend were becoming increasingly meaningful. The house, once a place of uncertainty, now felt like a home filled with love and joy.

As December continued, Lila began preparing for the upcoming Christmas holiday. She wanted to create a special celebration for the kids, filled with the magic and warmth of the season. She spent time decorating the house with twinkling lights, festive garlands, and a beautiful Christmas tree. The kids were thrilled as they helped with the decorations, adding their own ornaments and creating a holiday atmosphere.

One evening, as they sat around the tree, Lila took a moment to reflect on how much had changed since their move. The challenges they had faced seemed distant now, replaced by a sense of belonging and happiness. The community had welcomed them with open arms, and their new life in Riverbend was starting to feel like a dream come true.

On Christmas Eve, the Storm family attended a local holiday event—a candlelight service at the town's historic church. The church, adorned with beautiful decorations and illuminated by candlelight, provided a serene and festive atmosphere. The service included traditional carols and readings, and Lila felt a profound sense of peace as she listened to the music and shared the experience with her children.

After the service, they returned home and enjoyed a quiet evening together. They exchanged small gifts and shared their hopes and dreams for the coming year. The warmth and joy of the holiday season enveloped them, and Lila felt grateful for the new traditions they were creating and the sense of community they had found.

Christmas morning was a joyful occasion, with the kids eagerly opening presents and enjoying the excitement of the holiday. Lila had prepared a special breakfast, and they all sat down together to enjoy a festive meal. The day was filled with laughter, relaxation, and the simple pleasures of being together.

As the year drew to a close, Lila took time to reflect on the journey they had undertaken. The move to Riverbend had been a significant change, but it had also been an opportunity for growth and renewal. The challenges they had faced had been met with resilience and determination, and the rewards were evident in the happiness and sense of belonging they now experienced.

Lila was proud of how far they had come and looked forward to the new year with hope and excitement. The future was bright, and she felt confident that they were on the path to creating a fulfilling and meaningful life in their new home.

As the final days of December passed, the Storm family embraced the coming year with optimism and anticipation. They had built a solid foundation in Riverbend, and the possibilities for the future seemed endless. With each day, they continued to weave their own story, filled with new experiences, connections, and the promise of a bright and joyful future.

And so, with the arrival of the new year, Lila and her children stepped forward into the future, ready to embrace whatever came their way and build upon the life they had begun to create together.

Chapter 5: New Challenges

January brought with it a new year and a fresh set of opportunities and challenges for the Storm family. The cold winter days were a stark contrast to the warmth of the holiday season, but Lila was determined to maintain the positive momentum they had built over the past few months.

The new year began with a flurry of activity. Chloe, Lucas, and Jaxon were back in school and settling into their routines after the holiday break. Lila continued her efforts to integrate into the community, attending local events and getting involved in various activities. The transition to the new year was a chance to build on the progress they had made and face new challenges head-on.

One of the first hurdles was dealing with the unpredictable winter weather. The snow and ice created difficult driving conditions, and Lila found herself navigating a series of minor setbacks. Her car slipped on an icy patch one morning, resulting in a minor accident that left her car in need of repairs. It was a frustrating situation, but Lila managed to stay positive and organized a temporary solution to get around while her car was being fixed.

Despite the challenges, Lila was determined not to let them dampen her spirits. She used the extra time at home to focus on organizing and decluttering the house. It was a productive way to pass the time, and it also allowed her to make the home more comfortable and functional for her family.

As the days went by, Lila noticed that the kids were adjusting well to their new routines, but she also observed that they were experiencing some growing pains. Chloe was struggling with her schoolwork and feeling overwhelmed by the pressure to keep up with her peers. Lucas was having difficulty staying focused in class, and Jaxon was experiencing a lack of motivation with his art projects.

Lila decided to address these issues by talking to each of them individually and offering support. She reached out to Chloe's teachers to understand what additional help might be available and arranged for extra tutoring sessions. For Lucas, she worked on creating a more structured study routine and encouraged him to set small, achievable goals. With Jaxon, she explored new creative outlets and encouraged him to participate in local art workshops.

The adjustments were gradual, but Lila was pleased to see some improvement. Chloe's confidence began to build with the extra help, Lucas started to show more focus and enthusiasm, and Jaxon rediscovered his passion for art. It was clear that the support and encouragement from his family were making a difference.

In addition to managing the challenges at home, Lila also took on a new project—volunteering at the local food bank. She had heard about the organization through community events and felt it was a meaningful way to give back and become more involved in Riverbend. Volunteering at the food bank not only provided a sense of fulfillment but also allowed Lila to meet new people and build connections in the community.

One afternoon at the food bank, Lila met a woman named Karen, who had recently moved to Riverbend as well. Karen was friendly and enthusiastic, and the two quickly struck up a conversation. They discovered that they had a lot in common, including a shared passion for community service. Karen invited Lila to join a local book club, which she thought would be a great way for Lila to meet more people and engage in a new activity.

Lila accepted the invitation and attended the book club's next meeting. It was a lively and engaging group, and Lila enjoyed the discussions and the chance to connect with others who shared her interests. The book club became a regular and enjoyable part of her routine, offering both intellectual stimulation and social interaction.

As February arrived, the cold weather persisted, but Lila and her family continued to adapt and thrive. They spent time together in the cozy warmth of their home, enjoying indoor activities like board games, movie nights, and cooking new recipes. The garden was dormant during the winter months, but Lila used the time to plan for the upcoming spring and dream about new projects and improvements.

The winter season also brought a series of community events, including a winter carnival and a local charity auction. Lila and the kids participated in the events, contributing to the town's vibrant social scene and enjoying the opportunities to bond with their neighbors.

One Saturday, Lila decided to take the kids ice skating at a nearby rink. It was a fun and invigorating experience, and the kids were excited to try something new. They wobbled and laughed as they skated around the rink, and Lila joined in, savoring the simple joy of spending quality time together.

As the winter began to fade and the first signs of spring appeared, Lila reflected on the past few months with a sense of accomplishment. The challenges they had faced had tested their resilience, but they had emerged stronger and more connected. The new year had brought both obstacles and opportunities, and the Storm family had navigated them with determination and optimism.

Lila was proud of the progress they had made and looked forward to the arrival of spring. The garden would soon come back to life, and with it, a new chapter of their journey in Riverbend. The experiences and connections they had made in the past year had laid a solid foundation for the future, and Lila was excited to see what new adventures awaited them.

As February drew to a close, the promise of spring was on the horizon, bringing with it the hope of renewal and growth. Lila and her family were ready to embrace the changes and continue building the life they had envisioned in their new home.

MARCH ARRIVED WITH a hint of spring, teasing the arrival of warmer days and the promise of new beginnings. The snow had mostly melted away, leaving behind muddy patches and the first signs of green peeking through the soil. Lila used the changing season as an opportunity to start fresh and address a new set of goals and aspirations for her family.

One of her primary focuses was to encourage the kids to get involved in more community activities. The spring season brought a variety of events and opportunities, and Lila wanted to ensure that Chloe, Lucas, and Jaxon had a chance to explore their interests and make new friends.

Chloe had expressed an interest in joining the local theater group, which was preparing for a spring production of "Anne of Green Gables." Lila arranged for Chloe to audition, and Chloe was excited and nervous about the opportunity. After a few weeks of rehearsals, Chloe was cast in a supporting role, and her enthusiasm for the theater grew. Lila attended every rehearsal and performance, cheering Chloe on and marveling at her daughter's newfound confidence and talent.

Lucas had developed a fascination with nature and the environment. Lila found out about a local environmental club that organized clean-up events and educational workshops. Lucas eagerly joined the group, participating in river clean-ups and learning about conservation. The club became a source of pride for him, and he enjoyed sharing what he learned with his family.

Jaxon, meanwhile, was exploring his artistic side with a renewed sense of purpose. The local art center offered spring art classes, and Jaxon enrolled in a workshop focused on mixed media. His creativity flourished, and he began working on a series of paintings that he hoped to display at the upcoming community art show.

As the days grew longer and the weather warmed, Lila decided to take advantage of the improving conditions by focusing on the garden. She prepared the soil, planted early seeds, and began envisioning the garden's potential. The kids eagerly joined her, helping to clear the last of the winter debris and prepare the beds for new growth. The process was a bonding experience, and Lila enjoyed watching their excitement as they anticipated the coming spring.

In addition to the garden, Lila had another project in mind: renovating the basement to create a more functional space for the family. The basement had been largely unused, but Lila saw potential for it to become a playroom, a study area, and a space for creative activities. She began planning the renovation, researching ideas, and getting quotes from local contractors.

The renovation project quickly became a family effort. Chloe, Lucas, and Jaxon were all involved in various aspects of the project, from painting the walls to assembling furniture. The work was a great way for them to spend time together and contribute to making their home more enjoyable.

Amidst the busy schedule of activities and projects, Lila also made time to address her own goals. She continued her volunteer work at the food bank, which remained a fulfilling and important part of her life. She also decided to take a course on creative writing at the local community college, fulfilling a long-held dream of exploring her own writing.

Spring break arrived, and Lila planned a family trip to explore some of the nearby attractions. They visited a nature reserve, hiked along scenic trails, and enjoyed picnicking by a beautiful lake. The trip was a welcome break from their routine and provided a chance to relax and enjoy each other's company.

During the trip, the family reflected on the changes they had experienced since moving to Riverbend. They talked about their favorite moments and the new friendships they had made. It was clear that they had embraced their new life with enthusiasm and resilience.

As the days of spring continued to unfold, the Storm family settled into their new routines with a sense of satisfaction. The garden began to bloom, the renovation project took shape, and each of them found fulfillment in their pursuits. The challenges they had faced over the past year had strengthened their bonds and deepened their connection to their new community.

April brought with it the excitement of the community art show, where Jaxon proudly displayed his paintings. The event was a celebration of local talent, and Jaxon's work was well-received by the attendees. Lila felt immense pride as she watched Jaxon interact with other artists and receive compliments on his creations.

Chloe's theater production also reached its climax with the opening night of "Anne of Green Gables." Her performance was a hit, and the support from her family and friends made the experience even more special. Lila was amazed at how much Chloe had grown through her involvement in the theater.

Lucas continued to thrive in the environmental club, and his dedication to conservation was evident in the projects he participated in. Lila admired his commitment and was proud of the positive impact he was making in the community.

As spring transitioned into summer, Lila looked forward to the new experiences and opportunities that awaited them. The garden was flourishing, the basement renovation was nearing completion, and the kids were actively engaged in their interests. The Storm family had embraced their new life in Riverbend with open hearts and minds, and the future held endless possibilities.

With each passing day, Lila felt a growing sense of belonging and fulfillment. The journey had been transformative, and the experiences they had shared had enriched their lives. As the summer sun warmed their days, Lila and her family eagerly anticipated the adventures and opportunities that lay ahead, ready to continue building their life in Riverbend and creating memories that would last a lifetime.

AS THE CALENDAR TURNED to May, Riverbend was alive with the vibrancy of spring. The Storm family continued to thrive amidst the renewal of their surroundings. The garden was in full bloom, and Lila's basement renovation project was nearly complete, promising a versatile and inviting space for the family.

One Saturday, as they were putting the finishing touches on the basement, Lila received a call from Mrs. Reynolds. She had heard about a local community fair that was happening the following weekend and suggested that the Storm family participate. The fair would feature local artisans, food vendors, and various activities for families.

Excited by the prospect of another community event, Lila discussed it with the kids. Chloe, Lucas, and Jaxon were enthusiastic about the idea. Chloe volunteered to help with a booth for the theater group, Lucas was keen to assist with an environmental awareness station, and Jaxon was excited to display some of his artwork.

The week leading up to the fair was a whirlwind of preparation. Chloe prepared materials to promote the theater group's upcoming production. Lucas organized information about local environmental initiatives, while Jaxon selected his favorite pieces to showcase. Lila helped with logistical arrangements, ensuring that their participation would be both organized and enjoyable.

The day of the fair arrived with clear skies and warm temperatures. The community park was filled with tents, booths, and the sounds of laughter and chatter. The Storm family set up their booths and quickly became part of the lively atmosphere.

Chloe's booth was a hit with visitors, drawing attention to the theater group's activities and upcoming performances. She interacted with community members, handing out flyers and talking about the importance of local arts programs.

Lucas's environmental station was a focal point for those interested in conservation. He handed out informational brochures, engaged in discussions about local environmental issues, and even organized a small recycling drive. His enthusiasm was contagious, and he received praise for his efforts.

Jaxon's art display attracted a lot of attention. His paintings were well-received by fairgoers, and he enjoyed talking about his creative process and inspiration. His confidence grew with each positive comment, and he felt a deep sense of accomplishment.

The fair was a resounding success for the Storm family. They had not only contributed to the community but also enjoyed the opportunity to showcase their individual talents and interests. Lila felt a profound sense of pride as she watched her children interact with the community and receive recognition for their efforts.

As the fair wound down, Lila took a moment to reflect on how much had changed since their move to Riverbend. The family had embraced new opportunities, forged meaningful connections, and made a positive impact on their community. The sense of belonging they had achieved was a testament to their resilience and adaptability.

As summer approached, the Storm family looked forward to the season's activities. The completion of the basement renovation was a milestone, providing a new space for family activities and relaxation. The kids were excited to use the area for their various interests—Chloe for rehearsals and auditions, Lucas for his environmental projects, and Jaxon for his art.

The arrival of June brought with it the start of summer vacation. Lila planned a series of activities to keep the kids engaged and entertained. They organized family outings, including trips to nearby nature trails, a visit to a local water park, and a camping trip in the nearby mountains.

One weekend, Lila decided to host a summer barbecue for their friends and neighbors. She wanted to celebrate the successful completion of the basement renovation and the progress they had made since moving to Riverbend. The barbecue was a lively event, filled with good food, laughter, and the joy of spending time with loved ones.

The summer was a time of relaxation and enjoyment for the Storm family. They took advantage of the warm weather and longer days to create lasting memories together. The garden flourished, providing fresh vegetables and herbs for their meals, and the basement became a central hub for family activities and creativity.

As July drew to a close, Lila and her children continued to relish their summer adventures. The sense of fulfillment and happiness that had grown over the past year was evident in their daily lives. The challenges they had faced were behind them, and the future held the promise of continued growth and new experiences.

With the start of the new school year approaching, Lila began to prepare for the changes that would come with it. The kids were excited to return to school and continue pursuing their interests and goals. Lila felt confident that they were ready for the next chapter in their journey.

As summer gave way to the early days of autumn, the Storm family looked forward to the opportunities and challenges that awaited them. They had embraced their new life in Riverbend with open hearts and minds, and their experiences had strengthened their bond as a family.

Lila's reflections on their journey filled her with a sense of pride and gratitude. The move to Riverbend had been transformative, and the connections they had made and the accomplishments they had achieved were a testament to their resilience and determination.

With the promise of a new season on the horizon, the Storm family was ready to embrace whatever came next, knowing that they had the strength and unity to face any challenge and seize every opportunity that life had to offer.

Chapter 6: New Beginnings

August arrived, bringing with it the end of summer and the beginning of a new chapter for the Storm family. The end of summer break was met with a mix of excitement and apprehension as the kids prepared to return to school and Lila geared up for the changes that the new school year would bring.

Lila took the opportunity to have a family meeting to discuss their plans for the upcoming year. They reviewed the goals and activities they had set for themselves and talked about any adjustments they wanted to make. The discussion was both practical and heartfelt, as they reflected on their progress and shared their hopes for the future.

Chloe was excited about returning to school, particularly because she had been chosen to participate in a special theater program that would run through the school year. The program promised to be a great opportunity for her to hone her acting skills and work on more complex productions. Lila was supportive and proud of Chloe's dedication to the arts.

Lucas was looking forward to continuing his involvement in the environmental club. He had also expressed interest in starting a community garden project at school, which he hoped would engage more students in environmental stewardship. Lila encouraged Lucas to present his idea to the school administration and offered to help him with the proposal.

Jaxon was eager to start the new school year as well, especially because he had been selected to join an advanced art class. The class would allow him to explore new techniques and work on more ambitious projects. Jaxon was thrilled about the opportunity and felt motivated to push his creative boundaries.

As the kids prepared for school, Lila used the last few weeks of summer to organize the household and make any final adjustments. The basement renovation was complete, and she took the time to set up the space for maximum functionality. The playroom was stocked with toys and games, the study area was equipped with desks and supplies, and the art space was ready for Jaxon's projects.

In addition to preparing the house, Lila made sure to schedule some quality family time before the school year began. They spent a day at a local amusement park, enjoying rides and attractions, and another day exploring a nearby historical site. The outings were a great way to create lasting memories and enjoy each other's company before the busy school schedule took over.

The first day of school arrived with a sense of anticipation and nervous excitement. Chloe, Lucas, and Jaxon each set off for their respective schools with new backpacks and fresh school supplies. Lila waved them off, feeling a mix of pride and sentimentality as she watched them head into the new school year.

The first few weeks of school were filled with adjustments as the kids settled into their new routines. Chloe immersed herself in the theater program, rehearsing for her role and participating in workshops. She quickly became a key player in the program, gaining confidence and skill with each performance.

Lucas began working on his community garden project, collaborating with his teachers and classmates to bring his vision to life. The project was met with enthusiasm, and Lucas found himself energized by the positive response from the school community. His efforts were not only making a difference but also strengthening his leadership and organizational skills.

Jaxon thrived in his advanced art class, experimenting with new techniques and developing his portfolio. His passion for art grew stronger, and he began to explore different styles and mediums. His teacher praised his progress and encouraged him to consider participating in local art exhibitions.

With the kids busy with their school activities, Lila found herself with more time to focus on her own projects. She continued her creative writing course, which had become a fulfilling and inspiring outlet for her. She also dedicated time to her volunteer work at the food bank, finding joy in giving back to the community.

The autumn months were filled with school events and community activities. Chloe's theater program had several performances, and Lila attended each one, cheering her daughter on and marveling at her growth as an actress. Lucas's community garden project gained momentum, and he organized a successful harvest festival to celebrate the first crops. Jaxon's art was featured in a local gallery, where he received recognition for his work and had the chance to connect with other artists.

As October approached, Riverbend was transformed by the colors of fall. The trees were ablaze with red and orange leaves, and the crisp air was filled with the scent of autumn. Lila decided to host a fall-themed family gathering, inviting friends and neighbors to celebrate the season and enjoy the bounty of their garden.

The gathering was a delightful success, with homemade apple cider, pumpkin pie, and a variety of seasonal dishes. The kids shared their achievements and experiences, and Lila felt a deep sense of satisfaction as she looked around at the warmth and camaraderie of the gathering.

As the year continued to unfold, the Storm family embraced the opportunities and challenges that came their way. The sense of accomplishment and fulfillment they had experienced since moving to Riverbend continued to grow, and they looked forward to the new experiences that awaited them.

With each passing day, Lila felt grateful for the progress they had made and the life they had built in their new community. The journey had been transformative, and the future held the promise of continued growth and happiness.

As the end of the year approached, Lila and her family reflected on their journey with a sense of pride and anticipation. They had faced challenges, embraced new opportunities, and created a life filled with meaning and connection. With the promise of the future ahead, they were ready to face whatever came their way, united and hopeful for the adventures that awaited them in the coming year.

AS NOVEMBER SETTLED in, the days grew shorter and the air colder, signaling the approach of the holiday season. The Storm family was already feeling the excitement of the season's festivities, and Lila was eager to create new traditions that would bring warmth and joy to their home.

One of Lila's goals for the upcoming holidays was to organize a Thanksgiving dinner that would bring together friends and neighbors. She wanted to celebrate their newfound sense of community and express her gratitude for the support they had received throughout the year. The dinner would be a chance for them to connect with those who had become important in their lives.

Lila spent the weeks leading up to Thanksgiving planning the menu, decorating the house, and preparing for the event. She involved the kids in the preparations, making it a fun and collaborative effort. Chloe helped with setting up the dining area and designing festive place cards, while Lucas and Jaxon contributed by preparing some of the dishes and creating handmade decorations.

The day of Thanksgiving arrived, and the house was filled with the aroma of roasting turkey, freshly baked pies, and the warmth of holiday cheer. Lila had set a beautiful table adorned with autumn leaves and candles, creating a cozy and inviting atmosphere. Friends and neighbors began to arrive, each bringing a dish to share and contributing to the festive spirit.

The gathering was a heartwarming success. Lila felt a deep sense of fulfillment as she watched her family and friends come together, sharing stories, laughter, and a delicious meal. The conversations were lively, and the connections formed over the past year were evident in the genuine camaraderie and support that filled the room.

As December approached, the focus shifted to preparing for the winter holidays. Lila and the kids decorated the house with twinkling lights, garlands, and a beautifully adorned Christmas tree. They also participated in a local holiday charity drive, collecting toys and gifts for families in need. The act of giving back was a meaningful way to embrace the spirit of the season and reinforce their commitment to community.

The holiday season was a time of reflection and celebration for the Storm family. They enjoyed festive activities, including baking cookies, attending holiday performances, and taking part in a local winter festival. Each event was a chance to create lasting memories and enjoy the season's magic.

One of the highlights of the holiday season was the annual Riverbend Winter Festival, which featured ice skating, a holiday market, and a tree lighting ceremony. The Storm family attended the festival together, reveling in the festive atmosphere and enjoying the various activities. Chloe performed in a holiday-themed theater show, Lucas participated in a winter environmental clean-up event, and Jaxon's art was featured in a holiday exhibit.

As the year drew to a close, Lila took some time to reflect on the changes and growth the family had experienced since moving to Riverbend. The challenges they had faced had been met with resilience and determination, and the opportunities they had embraced had enriched their lives in countless ways.

The New Year's Eve celebration was a quiet yet meaningful affair at home. Lila and the kids gathered around to share their highlights of the year and their hopes for the future. They made a tradition of writing down their resolutions and goals for the coming year, each one sharing their personal aspirations and commitments.

The transition into the new year was marked by a sense of renewal and optimism. Lila felt confident in the path they had forged and excited for the opportunities that lay ahead. The Storm family had built a strong foundation in Riverbend, and they were ready to embrace the new year with enthusiasm and hope.

As January began, the Storm family returned to their routines with renewed energy and focus. The start of the new year brought fresh possibilities and a continued commitment to their goals and interests. Chloe continued to thrive in her theater program, Lucas worked on expanding his community garden project, and Jaxon pursued new artistic endeavors.

Lila remained dedicated to her writing and volunteer work, finding fulfillment in both. She continued to balance her various responsibilities while nurturing her personal passions and interests.

The winter months were a time of continued growth and reflection. The Storm family remained engaged in their community, supporting each other's endeavors and celebrating their successes. They looked forward to the coming year with a sense of excitement and anticipation, eager to continue their journey in Riverbend and embrace the adventures that awaited them.

As the snow began to fall and the landscape transformed into a winter wonderland, Lila and her family took comfort in the knowledge that they had built a life filled with connection, purpose, and joy. The challenges of the past year had strengthened their bonds and prepared them for whatever the future held. With each new day, they embraced the promise of the new year and the opportunities it would bring.

JANUARY'S CHILL BROUGHT with it a sense of new beginnings and fresh opportunities for the Storm family. The post-holiday lull gave them a chance to settle into their routines and reflect on their progress while preparing for the upcoming months.

One Saturday morning, Lila was in the kitchen, preparing a pot of hearty soup. The kitchen had become a central hub of activity, where the family gathered not only to eat but to share their thoughts and ideas. The aroma of the soup filled the room, providing a comforting backdrop to their discussion.

Chloe walked in, her face glowing with excitement. "Mom, I've been thinking about starting a new project for the theater group. What if we created a community arts festival? It could be a great way to involve more people and showcase local talent."

Lila looked up from her chopping board, her interest piqued. "That sounds like a wonderful idea, Chloe. How would you like to get started?"

Chloe explained her vision: a festival that would bring together performers, artists, and artisans from Riverbend and the surrounding areas. She wanted to include workshops, live performances, and art displays. Lila could see Chloe's passion for the project and was eager to support her.

"Why don't you draft a plan and present it to your theater group's board? I can help you with the logistics and promotion once you get the green light," Lila suggested.

Chloe beamed. "Thanks, Mom. I'll get started on it right away."

Lucas, meanwhile, was busy working on his community garden project. The enthusiasm he had shown for the garden at school had blossomed into a broader initiative. He had begun working on a proposal for a community greenhouse that could provide fresh produce year-round. He spent his weekends researching greenhouse designs and talking to local horticulturists.

"I want this greenhouse to be a place where people can learn about gardening and grow their own food," Lucas said one evening, showing Lila his plans.

Lila was impressed with his dedication. "Your vision is inspiring, Lucas. Have you thought about reaching out to local businesses for sponsorship or support?"

Lucas nodded. "Yes, I'm planning to start with a few local garden centers and maybe some businesses that focus on sustainability."

Jaxon was equally engaged in his artistic pursuits. He was working on a new series of paintings inspired by the winter landscape. His recent work had gained attention at the local art gallery, and he was now exploring ideas for a solo exhibition.

"I've been thinking about creating a series that reflects the changing seasons," Jaxon said, showing Lila a few of his sketches. "I want to capture the beauty of winter and how it transforms into spring."

Lila admired his creativity. "That sounds like a fantastic concept, Jaxon. Maybe you could even include some interactive elements in your exhibition, like a live painting demonstration or workshops for kids."

As January progressed, the Storm family continued to balance their individual projects with family activities. They enjoyed cozy evenings by the fireplace, played board games, and shared stories about their days. The winter weather, while cold, provided an opportunity for them to appreciate the comfort of home and each other's company.

Chloe's community arts festival proposal was met with enthusiasm from the theater group's board. With Lila's help, Chloe began planning the festival, reaching out to local artists and performers, securing venues, and organizing promotional materials. The project quickly gained momentum, and Chloe's excitement was palpable as the festival date approached.

Lucas's greenhouse proposal was also making progress. He had secured a few initial sponsors and was working on finalizing the design and securing a location. The support from the community was encouraging, and Lucas was motivated by the positive response to his vision.

Jaxon's art series began to take shape, and he was busy preparing for his exhibition. He set up a small studio space in the basement, where he worked on his paintings and experimented with new techniques. The upcoming exhibition was a source of both anticipation and nerves, but Jaxon was determined to make it a success.

As February arrived, the Storm family's projects were gaining momentum, and their individual pursuits were starting to take shape. The community arts festival, the greenhouse project, and Jaxon's exhibition were all moving forward, each contributing to the family's sense of purpose and achievement.

The winter season continued to provide a backdrop of introspection and growth. The Storm family embraced the challenges and opportunities that came their way, supporting each other through their individual endeavors while strengthening their bonds as a family.

With each passing day, Lila felt a deep sense of gratitude for the life they had built in Riverbend. The journey had been filled with moments of joy, accomplishment, and connection. As the cold of winter began to give way to the first hints of spring, the Storm family looked forward to the new adventures and experiences that awaited them.

Their projects were not only personal milestones but also opportunities to contribute to their community and make a positive impact. The upcoming months promised to be filled with continued growth, collaboration, and the joy of seeing their visions come to fruition. With hope and excitement, the Storm family embraced the new year and the possibilities it held, ready to face whatever challenges and opportunities lay ahead.

Chapter 7: Winter's End

February in Riverbend was a blend of cold winds and emerging signs of spring. Snow still blanketed the town, but the days were growing longer, and the occasional warm spell hinted at the approaching change of seasons. For the Storm family, the end of winter marked the culmination of several projects and the beginning of new opportunities.

Chloe's community arts festival was rapidly approaching. The planning was in full swing, and Chloe was immersed in finalizing details. She had secured a venue at a local park and was busy coordinating with vendors, performers, and artists. Her excitement was infectious, and she often talked about the festival's potential to bring the community together and showcase local talent.

Lila was deeply involved in helping Chloe with the festival. They spent evenings working on promotional materials, finalizing the schedule, and organizing logistics. Chloe's enthusiasm for the project was a source of inspiration for Lila, and she was proud of her daughter's dedication and hard work.

Lucas's greenhouse project was also making strides. He had successfully secured more sponsorships and had begun the groundwork for the greenhouse's construction. Local businesses were offering support, and the project was becoming a community effort. Lucas spent his weekends working on-site, overseeing the progress and ensuring that the project stayed on track.

Jaxon's art exhibition was nearing its opening, and he was busy preparing for the event. His studio was filled with completed paintings, and he worked tirelessly to finalize the details of the exhibition. The anticipation was building, and Jaxon was excited about sharing his work with the community. He had also planned a live painting demonstration as part of the exhibition, which he hoped would engage and inspire visitors.

As February progressed, the Storm family faced a series of final preparations and events. Chloe's festival was scheduled for mid-month, Lucas's greenhouse was set to open its doors by the end of the month, and Jaxon's art exhibition was scheduled for a weekend in between. It was a busy time, but the family was energized by the momentum of their projects.

One Friday evening, Lila decided to host a small gathering to celebrate the progress they had made. She invited friends, neighbors, and local supporters to their home for a casual dinner and informal preview of the upcoming events. The gathering was a chance to thank everyone for their support and share their excitement about the projects.

The evening was filled with lively conversations, laughter, and a sense of camaraderie. Chloe spoke about the festival and her vision for it, Lucas talked about the greenhouse and its potential impact on the community, and Jaxon shared his artistic journey and the inspiration behind his exhibition.

The support and encouragement from their friends and neighbors were heartwarming. It was clear that the Storm family's efforts were making a positive impact, and the sense of community was palpable.

The day of Chloe's community arts festival arrived with clear skies and a hint of spring in the air. The park was transformed into a vibrant space filled with booths, performances, and activities. Chloe and her team worked tirelessly to ensure everything was in place, and the festival began with a lively opening ceremony.

The festival was a resounding success. Local artists and performers showcased their talents, and visitors enjoyed a variety of workshops, live music, and art displays. Chloe's vision had come to life, and the community embraced the event with enthusiasm and support. Lila watched with pride as Chloe interacted with attendees and celebrated the achievements of the festival.

A week later, Lucas's greenhouse project held its grand opening. The event was well-attended, and the greenhouse was a source of pride for the community. Lucas's hard work and dedication were evident in the greenhouse's design and functionality. The opening marked a significant milestone, and Lucas was excited to see the positive impact the greenhouse would have on the community.

Jaxon's art exhibition followed shortly after. The gallery was filled with visitors eager to see Jaxon's work. The live painting demonstration was a highlight of the event, drawing attention and praise from the attendees. Jaxon felt a sense of accomplishment as he shared his art and connected with others who appreciated his work.

With their major projects complete, the Storm family took some time to relax and enjoy the results of their hard work. The winter weather began to give way to the first signs of spring, and the family took advantage of the milder temperatures to spend more time outdoors.

One Saturday afternoon, Lila and the kids went for a hike in the nearby nature reserve. The trails were beginning to thaw, and the early signs of spring were visible in the budding trees and emerging flowers. The hike was a refreshing change of pace, and the family enjoyed the chance to reconnect with nature and each other.

As March unfolded, the Storm family looked forward to the arrival of spring with a sense of anticipation and renewal. The projects they had worked on were now part of the community's fabric, and they were ready to Chapter 8: Spring Awakening

April arrived with a burst of color and warmth, transforming Riverbend into a vibrant tapestry of blooming flowers and budding trees. The Storm family embraced the season of renewal with enthusiasm, each member looking forward to new opportunities and personal growth.

Chloe's regional arts network event, which she had been working on for months, was just around the corner. She was excited but also nervous, as this event would be her biggest undertaking yet. The goal was to bring together artists, performers, and community members from across the region to share their work and foster collaboration. Chloe had organized a series of workshops, panel discussions, and showcases, all designed to celebrate and elevate local talent.

Lila supported Chloe in the final preparations, helping with logistics and ensuring that every detail was accounted for. The night before the event, they stayed up late finalizing the program and making sure everything was ready. Chloe's determination and passion were evident, and Lila felt immense pride in her daughter's dedication.

The day of the event arrived with clear skies and a gentle breeze, perfect for the outdoor components of the festival. The park was transformed into a lively venue, with booths, stages, and art installations spread out across the grounds. Chloe's hard work paid off as the festival began, drawing a diverse crowd eager to experience the range of artistic offerings.

The event was a resounding success. Local artists showcased their work, performers captivated the audience, and workshops were well-attended. Chloe's vision had come to life, and the positive feedback from participants and attendees was a testament to her efforts. Lila watched with pride as Chloe engaged with the community, celebrating the achievements of the festival and forging new connections.

Lucas's greenhouse project reached a significant milestone with its first harvest. The community eagerly anticipated the fresh produce, and Lucas organized a harvest festival to celebrate the occasion. The event included cooking demonstrations, a farmer's market, and educational talks on sustainable gardening. Lucas's hard work had paid off, and the greenhouse had become a cornerstone of the community's commitment to sustainability.

Jaxon continued to explore new artistic endeavors, inspired by the changing season. His new series of paintings, reflecting the vibrant colors and themes of spring, was well-received at a local art fair. Jaxon's work was displayed alongside other emerging artists, and he enjoyed the opportunity to network and share his creative process with others.

With the arrival of spring, the Storm family also took time to enjoy the outdoors. They participated in community events, took weekend hikes, and made the most of the pleasant weather. The sense of renewal and growth was evident in their daily lives, and they relished the opportunities to connect with nature and each other.

One sunny afternoon, Lila decided to host a family picnic at the park. It was a chance for them to relax and enjoy a leisurely day together. They packed a basket with homemade treats and set up a picnic blanket under a shady tree. As they ate and chatted, the warmth of the season and the sense of togetherness made for a perfect day.

As May approached, the Storm family prepared for the final events of their spring projects. Chloe was working on the follow-up to the arts network event, aiming to create a sustainable platform for ongoing artistic collaboration. Lucas continued to develop the greenhouse project, exploring ways to expand its impact and reach more community members. Jaxon was planning his next exhibition, inspired by the beauty of the season and eager to share his latest work with a broader audience.

The transition from winter to spring had been a period of significant growth and achievement for the Storm family. They had embraced new opportunities, supported each other's goals, and built a strong foundation in their community. As they looked forward to the summer months, they felt a deep sense of accomplishment and anticipation for the future.

Lila reflected on the journey they had undertaken, appreciating the resilience and determination that had brought them to this point. The changes and challenges of the past year had shaped their experiences and strengthened their bonds. With the arrival of spring, the Storm family was ready to embrace the next chapter of their lives with optimism and excitement.

As the days grew warmer and the world continued to bloom, the Storm family faced the future with renewed energy and hope. They were eager to build on their successes, explore new opportunities, and continue making a positive impact in Riverbend. The season of renewal had brought them closer together and inspired them to look ahead with confidence and enthusiasm.

the new opportunities and experiences that the coming months would bring.

The success of their endeavors had strengthened their sense of belonging in Riverbend and reaffirmed their commitment to making a positive impact. As the snow melted and the days grew longer, the Storm family welcomed the change of seasons with optimism and excitement for the future.

AS MARCH CAME INTO full swing, Riverbend began to shake off the last vestiges of winter. The snow had receded, giving way to patches of green and the first blooms of the season. For the Storm family, this transition marked a period of both reflection and forward momentum.

Chloe's community arts festival had not only been a success but had also sparked interest in similar events across the region. She received several inquiries from neighboring towns interested in replicating the festival's model. Energized by this response, Chloe began planning a follow-up project: a regional arts network aimed at connecting local artists and performers with broader audiences.

Lucas's greenhouse was thriving, and it became a focal point for community engagement. He organized workshops on sustainable gardening and led tours for local school groups. The greenhouse was not only a source of fresh produce but also a hub for education and community building. Lucas was proud to see his project making a tangible difference.

Jaxon's art exhibition had been well-received, and he continued to explore new creative avenues. His work was gaining recognition, and he was invited to participate in a collaborative project with other local artists. This new opportunity allowed him to experiment with mixed media and expand his artistic repertoire.

Amidst these busy times, Lila decided to take a step back and reflect on the changes that had taken place over the past year. She had managed to balance her writing, volunteer work, and family responsibilities while supporting her children's endeavors. The sense of fulfillment she felt was a testament to the resilience and adaptability that had defined their journey.

One evening, as the family gathered for dinner, Lila proposed a special family retreat. She suggested spending a weekend at a cabin in the nearby mountains to unwind and reconnect. The idea was met with enthusiastic agreement, and the family began preparing for the getaway.

The weekend at the cabin was a much-needed escape from their busy routines. Nestled in a picturesque setting with panoramic views of the mountains, the cabin provided a serene backdrop for relaxation and togetherness. The family spent their days hiking, playing games, and enjoying the beauty of nature. It was a chance to recharge and appreciate the simple pleasures of life.

During the retreat, Lila and the kids had heartfelt conversations about their goals and dreams. Chloe shared her vision for the regional arts network, Lucas discussed his plans for expanding the greenhouse project, and Jaxon talked about his aspirations for future artistic collaborations. Each conversation was a reflection of their growth and the positive impact they were making on their community.

As the retreat came to an end, the Storm family returned to Riverbend with renewed energy and a deeper sense of connection. The experience had strengthened their bond and reaffirmed their commitment to supporting each other's dreams.

March continued with a flurry of activity. Chloe's regional arts network began to take shape, with the first networking event scheduled for the end of the month. Lucas's greenhouse project was preparing for its first harvest, and Jaxon was working on new pieces for an upcoming art fair.

With spring in full bloom, the Storm family embraced the season of renewal with enthusiasm. They participated in local events, supported each other's projects, and continued to build their lives in Riverbend. The sense of accomplishment and community they had cultivated was evident in their daily lives.

As April approached, Lila took a moment to reflect on the journey they had undertaken. The challenges they had faced, the opportunities they had embraced, and the connections they had forged were all part of a larger story of growth and transformation. The Storm family had found their place in Riverbend, and the future held the promise of continued adventure and fulfillment.

With the arrival of spring, the world outside mirrored the changes within. The days grew warmer, the flowers bloomed, and the promise of new beginnings was in the air. The Storm family looked forward to the season ahead with a sense of excitement and anticipation, ready to embrace the opportunities and experiences that awaited them.

As they continued to move forward, Lila and her children knew that their journey was far from over. The challenges and successes of the past year had paved the way for a future filled with possibility. With hope in their hearts and determination in their spirits, they faced the future with optimism and readiness for whatever lay ahead.

Chapter 8: Spring Awakening

April arrived with a burst of color and warmth, transforming Riverbend into a vibrant tapestry of blooming flowers and budding trees. The Storm family embraced the season of renewal with enthusiasm, each member looking forward to new opportunities and personal growth.

Chloe's regional arts network event, which she had been working on for months, was just around the corner. She was excited but also nervous, as this event would be her biggest undertaking yet. The goal was to bring together artists, performers, and community members from across the region to share their work and foster collaboration. Chloe had organized a series of workshops, panel discussions, and showcases, all designed to celebrate and elevate local talent.

Lila supported Chloe in the final preparations, helping with logistics and ensuring that every detail was accounted for. The night before the event, they stayed up late finalizing the program and making sure everything was ready. Chloe's determination and passion were evident, and Lila felt immense pride in her daughter's dedication.

The day of the event arrived with clear skies and a gentle breeze, perfect for the outdoor components of the festival. The park was transformed into a lively venue, with booths, stages, and art installations spread out across the grounds. Chloe's hard work paid off as the festival began, drawing a diverse crowd eager to experience the range of artistic offerings.

The event was a resounding success. Local artists showcased their work, performers captivated the audience, and workshops were well-attended. Chloe's vision had come to life, and the positive feedback from participants and attendees was a testament to her efforts. Lila watched with pride as Chloe engaged with the community, celebrating the achievements of the festival and forging new connections.

Lucas's greenhouse project reached a significant milestone with its first harvest. The community eagerly anticipated the fresh produce, and Lucas organized a harvest festival to celebrate the occasion. The event included cooking demonstrations, a farmer's market, and educational talks on sustainable gardening. Lucas's hard work had paid off, and the greenhouse had become a cornerstone of the community's commitment to sustainability.

Jaxon continued to explore new artistic endeavors, inspired by the changing season. His new series of paintings, reflecting the vibrant colors and themes of spring, was well-received at a local art fair. Jaxon's work was displayed alongside other emerging artists, and he enjoyed the opportunity to network and share his creative process with others.

With the arrival of spring, the Storm family also took time to enjoy the outdoors. They participated in community events, took weekend hikes, and made the most of the pleasant weather. The sense of renewal and growth was evident in their daily lives, and they relished the opportunities to connect with nature and each other.

One sunny afternoon, Lila decided to host a family picnic at the park. It was a chance for them to relax and enjoy a leisurely day together. They packed a basket with homemade treats and set up a picnic blanket under a shady tree. As they ate and chatted, the warmth of the season and the sense of togetherness made for a perfect day.

As May approached, the Storm family prepared for the final events of their spring projects. Chloe was working on the follow-up to the arts network event, aiming to create a sustainable platform for ongoing artistic collaboration. Lucas continued to develop the greenhouse project, exploring ways to expand its impact and reach more community members. Jaxon was planning his next exhibition, inspired by the beauty of the season and eager to share his latest work with a broader audience.

The transition from winter to spring had been a period of significant growth and achievement for the Storm family. They had embraced new opportunities, supported each other's goals, and built a strong foundation in their community. As they looked forward to the summer months, they felt a deep sense of accomplishment and anticipation for the future.

Lila reflected on the journey they had undertaken, appreciating the resilience and determination that had brought them to this point. The changes and challenges of the past year had shaped their experiences and strengthened their bonds. With the arrival of spring, the Storm family was ready to embrace the next chapter of their lives with optimism and excitement.

As the days grew warmer and the world continued to bloom, the Storm family faced the future with renewed energy and hope. They were eager to build on their successes, explore new opportunities, and continue making a positive impact in Riverbend. The season of renewal had brought them closer together and inspired them to look ahead with confidence and enthusiasm.

THE ARRIVAL OF MAY brought with it a sense of vitality and excitement. For the Storm family, this month was filled with anticipation and preparation as they neared the culmination of their spring projects and looked forward to the summer ahead.

Chloe's regional arts network had gained significant traction since the festival. She had been working diligently to turn the event's success into a sustainable initiative. She organized a series of follow-up meetings with artists and community leaders to discuss the formation of a permanent arts council. The goal was to create a platform that would continue to support local talent and foster collaboration among artists from various disciplines.

One evening, Chloe and Lila sat down to review the progress of the arts council. Chloe was excited about the possibilities, but also apprehensive about the challenges ahead.

"I've been thinking about how to keep the momentum going," Chloe said, her eyes focused on the plans spread out before her. "We need to establish a clear structure for the council and ensure we have enough support from the community."

Lila nodded. "You've already done a remarkable job bringing people together. The next steps will be challenging, but you have the skills and dedication to make it work. Perhaps you could start by forming a core team of committed volunteers to help with the administrative aspects."

Chloe took a deep breath, reassured by her mother's encouragement. "That's a great idea. I'll start reaching out to potential team members and outline our goals for the next few months."

Lucas was busy with the greenhouse's expansion plans. The success of the initial harvest had sparked interest from local schools and community organizations. Lucas was working on developing educational programs that would allow students and community members to learn about sustainable gardening and the benefits of locally grown produce.

On a bright Saturday morning, Lucas hosted a workshop for local schoolchildren. The greenhouse was abuzz with activity as the students learned about planting techniques, composting, and the importance of sustainable practices. Lucas's enthusiasm and expertise were evident, and the children were engaged and eager to learn.

"Seeing their excitement and curiosity is incredibly rewarding," Lucas said to Lila later that day. "I'm looking forward to expanding our programs and reaching even more people."

Lila smiled, proud of her son's dedication. "You're making a real difference in the community, Lucas. Keep up the great work."

Jaxon's preparations for his next art exhibition were in full swing. Inspired by the vibrant colors and themes of spring, he was working on a new series of paintings that captured the essence of the season. The upcoming exhibition was to be held at a larger gallery in a neighboring city, and Jaxon was excited about the opportunity to reach a broader audience.

He spent long hours in his studio, experimenting with new techniques and perfecting his pieces. The creative process was both challenging and fulfilling, and Jaxon found himself immersed in his work. He also planned to include a few interactive elements, such as live painting demonstrations and a Q&A session, to engage with visitors and share his artistic journey.

As May drew to a close, the Storm family celebrated the progress of their projects and the arrival of summer. They hosted a small gathering at their home to mark the end of the spring season and to express their gratitude for the support they had received from friends and neighbors.

The gathering was filled with laughter, good food, and heartfelt conversations. Chloe talked about the next steps for the arts council, Lucas shared his plans for the greenhouse's educational programs, and Jaxon excitedly discussed his upcoming exhibition. The sense of community and connection was palpable, and the support from their friends and neighbors was deeply appreciated.

The summer months promised to be a time of continued growth and exploration. Chloe's arts council was set to launch its first official programs, Lucas's greenhouse was preparing for its second harvest, and Jaxon's exhibition was just around the corner. The Storm family looked forward to the opportunities and adventures that awaited them, eager to build on their successes and make the most of the season.

As the first days of summer arrived, the Storm family embraced the warmth and energy of the season. They spent time outdoors, participating in local events, and enjoying the beauty of Riverbend. The sense of renewal and possibility was ever-present, and they faced the future with excitement and optimism.

The journey they had undertaken over the past year had brought them closer together and strengthened their connection to their community. With the arrival of summer, they were ready to embrace the next chapter of their lives with enthusiasm and a renewed sense of purpose. The adventures of the coming months awaited, and the Storm family was prepared to meet them with hope and determination.

AS JUNE BEGAN, RIVERBEND was in full swing with the energy of summer. The Storm family embraced the season with a mixture of excitement and anticipation. Each member was focused on their respective projects, looking forward to new milestones and opportunities.

Chloe's work on the regional arts council continued to gain momentum. She had successfully assembled a core team of volunteers who were passionate about supporting local artists and fostering creative collaboration. The council's first official meeting was scheduled for mid-June, and Chloe was busy preparing for it. She aimed to outline the council's mission, set goals for the coming year, and discuss potential funding sources.

In preparation for the meeting, Chloe organized a series of community outreach events to gather input from local artists and residents. She wanted to ensure that the council's initiatives would reflect the needs and desires of the community. These events included artist talks, open forums, and interactive workshops. The feedback she received was overwhelmingly positive, and it provided valuable insights into the direction the council should take.

Lucas was equally busy with the greenhouse. The second harvest was approaching, and he was expanding the greenhouse's impact by introducing new features. He had started a composting program and was working on a rainwater collection system to make the greenhouse more sustainable. Additionally, Lucas was planning a summer farmers' market to showcase the produce from the greenhouse and support local vendors.

The farmers' market was scheduled for the end of June, and Lucas was excited about the opportunity to engage with the community. He collaborated with local artisans and food producers to create a vibrant market that would offer fresh produce, handmade goods, and live entertainment. The event promised to be a highlight of the summer and a chance for Lucas to celebrate the greenhouse's success.

Jaxon's upcoming exhibition was also a source of excitement. The gallery in the neighboring city was preparing for the opening, and Jaxon was finalizing the details of his new series. The exhibition was to feature a collection of paintings inspired by the spring season, along with interactive elements that would allow visitors to engage with his creative process.

Jaxon had arranged for live painting sessions during the exhibition, where he would demonstrate his techniques and interact with attendees. He was eager to share his work and connect with art enthusiasts from outside Riverbend. The opportunity to showcase his art in a larger venue was a significant step in his artistic career.

As the day of Chloe's arts council meeting approached, she felt a mixture of excitement and nerves. She wanted the council to be a beacon of creativity and collaboration, and she was determined to make a positive impact. The meeting was held in the community center, and Chloe was pleased to see a diverse group of artists, performers, and residents in attendance.

The meeting was a success. Chloe and her team presented the council's mission and goals, and the feedback from attendees was constructive and supportive. The council's initiatives were well-received, and several community members volunteered to contribute their skills and resources.

The farmers' market, organized by Lucas, was a resounding success. The event drew a large crowd, and the market was filled with vibrant stalls, delicious food, and live music. The greenhouse's produce was a hit, and Lucas was thrilled to see the community's enthusiasm. The farmers' market not only showcased the greenhouse's impact but also strengthened local connections and supported small businesses.

Jaxon's art exhibition was another highlight of the summer. The opening night was a celebration of creativity, with visitors admiring Jaxon's work and participating in the live painting sessions. The exhibition received positive reviews, and Jaxon's interactive elements were well-received. It was a proud moment for Jaxon as he shared his art with a broader audience and engaged with fellow artists.

With the successes of Chloe's arts council, Lucas's farmers' market, and Jaxon's exhibition, the Storm family felt a deep sense of accomplishment. The summer had been a time of growth and celebration, and they were eager to continue building on their achievements.

As the days grew longer and the warmth of summer enveloped Riverbend, the Storm family took time to enjoy the season's simple pleasures. They spent weekends exploring the outdoors, participating in community events, and relishing the time they had together.

The arrival of summer marked a new chapter in their journey. The Storm family had embraced the challenges and opportunities of the past year with resilience and creativity. As they looked forward to the coming months, they felt a renewed sense of purpose and optimism.

The summer promised to be filled with new adventures and experiences. The Storm family was ready to embrace the future with hope and determination, continuing to make a positive impact on their community and support each other's dreams. The season of renewal and growth had brought them closer together, and they faced the future with excitement and anticipation.

Chapter 9: Summer's Embrace

July brought a wave of heat and energy to Riverbend, and the Storm family was immersed in the rhythms of summer. With the successes of their spring projects behind them, they were focused on new opportunities and savoring the season's vibrant atmosphere.

Chloe's arts council had begun to take shape, with a series of workshops and collaborative events scheduled throughout the summer. Her next major initiative was a community mural project designed to involve local artists and residents in creating a large-scale piece of public art. The mural would be painted on the side of a prominent downtown building, and Chloe hoped it would serve as both a visual representation of Riverbend's creative spirit and a catalyst for future artistic endeavors.

The mural project kicked off with a community meeting where Chloe presented her vision and invited local artists to contribute their ideas. The response was enthusiastic, and several artists expressed their interest in participating. Chloe and her team organized brainstorming sessions, design workshops, and planning meetings to ensure the project's success.

Lucas's greenhouse continued to thrive, and he was busy with the summer farmers' market, which had become a popular community event. The market had expanded to include a wider variety of vendors, and Lucas was working on integrating educational elements into the event, such as gardening demonstrations and sustainable living workshops. The market had become a hub of activity and a focal point for community engagement.

In addition to the market, Lucas was also involved in planning a summer garden tour. The tour would feature several local gardens, including the greenhouse's new composting system and rainwater collection features. Lucas hoped the tour would inspire others to adopt sustainable practices and appreciate the beauty of local gardens.

Jaxon's art exhibition had received widespread acclaim, and he was invited to participate in an art residency program in a nearby city. The residency offered him the opportunity to work in a dedicated studio space, collaborate with other artists, and showcase his work in a prominent gallery. Jaxon eagerly accepted the invitation, seeing it as a chance to further develop his artistic skills and expand his network.

As Jaxon prepared for the residency, he took time to reflect on his journey and the impact of his recent successes. He had been busy with preparations, including packing his artwork and organizing travel logistics. Despite the hectic schedule, he felt a deep sense of excitement and anticipation for the new experience.

One evening, the Storm family gathered for a barbecue at their home to celebrate their achievements and enjoy each other's company. The backyard was filled with the aroma of grilled food, the sound of laughter, and the warmth of summer's embrace. Chloe, Lucas, and Jaxon shared updates on their respective projects, and Lila expressed her pride in their accomplishments.

As the sun set and the stars began to emerge, the family sat around the fire pit, reminiscing about the past year and discussing their hopes for the future. The sense of unity and accomplishment was palpable, and they took a moment to appreciate the journey they had undertaken together.

The mural project progressed smoothly, with local artists and residents working side by side to bring the design to life. The mural depicted scenes of Riverbend's natural beauty, community spirit, and artistic diversity. As the painting continued, the excitement and involvement of the community grew, and the mural became a symbol of collective creativity and collaboration.

Lucas's summer garden tour was well-attended, and the event was a success. Participants toured several local gardens, including the greenhouse's new features, and engaged in discussions about sustainable gardening practices. The tour not only highlighted the importance of sustainability but also fostered a sense of community and shared purpose.

Jaxon's art residency proved to be a transformative experience. He immersed himself in his work, experimenting with new techniques and collaborating with fellow artists. The residency provided him with valuable feedback and inspiration, and he looked forward to sharing the results of his creative exploration in future exhibitions.

As July drew to a close, the Storm family reflected on the summer's accomplishments and the positive impact they had made in their community. The projects they had undertaken had not only enriched their lives but also strengthened their connection to Riverbend and its residents.

The warmth of summer continued to envelop Riverbend, and the Storm family embraced the season with gratitude and joy. They looked forward to the coming months with a sense of excitement and anticipation, ready to continue their journey of growth and discovery.

With their summer projects nearing completion and new opportunities on the horizon, the Storm family felt a renewed sense of purpose and unity. The season of summer had been a time of celebration, creativity, and connection, and they were eager to see what the future would bring as they continued to build on their successes and support each other's dreams.

AS AUGUST ARRIVED, Riverbend was at the height of summer, and the Storm family was deep into their respective projects. The warmth of the season was matched by the enthusiasm and commitment each member brought to their endeavors.

Chloe's community mural project was progressing beautifully. The wall, once a blank canvas, was now adorned with vivid colors and intricate designs that captured the essence of Riverbend. The mural depicted a blend of local landscapes, iconic landmarks, and abstract representations of the community's creativity. It had become a focal point for the town, and Chloe was thrilled to see the positive reaction from residents and visitors alike.

On a sunny afternoon, Chloe organized a mural unveiling event to celebrate the project's completion. The event was attended by many of the artists who had contributed to the mural, as well as local residents who had followed the project's progress. There was a sense of pride and accomplishment in the air as the mural was revealed to the crowd. Chloe spoke about the project's impact and thanked everyone who had been involved. The event concluded with live music and refreshments, creating a festive atmosphere.

Lucas's summer farmers' market continued to flourish. The market had become a beloved community event, offering fresh produce, handmade crafts, and live entertainment. Lucas had also introduced a series of educational workshops on topics such as organic gardening, composting, and food preservation. These workshops were well-attended and received positive feedback from participants who appreciated the opportunity to learn and engage with sustainable practices.

The summer garden tour, organized by Lucas, was another highlight. The tour featured a variety of local gardens, showcasing different approaches to sustainable gardening and landscape design. The event attracted gardening enthusiasts and community members who were inspired by the creativity and dedication of local gardeners. Lucas was pleased to see the enthusiasm and interest in sustainable practices, and he felt a sense of fulfillment in contributing to the community's appreciation of gardening.

Jaxon's art residency was drawing to a close, and he was preparing to return to Riverbend with new experiences and insights. The residency had been a transformative period for Jaxon, allowing him to explore new techniques, collaborate with other artists, and gain valuable feedback on his work. He was excited to share the results of his residency with his community and integrate the new ideas into his future projects.

Before leaving the residency, Jaxon organized a small exhibition of his recent work. The exhibition showcased a series of paintings and mixed media pieces inspired by his experiences during the residency. It was a chance for Jaxon to present his work to a broader audience and receive feedback from art enthusiasts and critics.

As the end of August approached, the Storm family took a moment to reflect on the summer's accomplishments and the impact they had made in their community. The mural project had become a symbol of artistic collaboration, the farmers' market had fostered community engagement and education, and Jaxon's residency had provided him with new creative opportunities.

One evening, the family gathered at their home for a quiet dinner, enjoying the late summer twilight and the company of one another. Chloe, Lucas, and Jaxon shared their reflections on their recent experiences and discussed their plans for the future. Lila listened with pride, appreciating the growth and achievements of her children.

"We've had an incredible summer," Chloe said, raising her glass. "Each of us has accomplished so much, and we've made a positive impact on our community."

Lucas nodded in agreement. "It's amazing to see how our projects have come together and how the community has responded. I'm excited to continue building on these experiences."

Jaxon smiled, feeling a sense of satisfaction. "The residency was a turning point for me, and I can't wait to bring what I've learned back to Riverbend. It's been a summer of growth and exploration."

Lila looked around the table, her heart full. "I'm so proud of each of you. The work you've done has not only enriched our lives but also strengthened our connections with the community. Here's to continued success and new adventures."

As they enjoyed their meal and the warm summer evening, the Storm family reflected on the journey they had undertaken and the possibilities that lay ahead. The season of summer had been a time of achievement, celebration, and renewal, and they looked forward to the coming months with optimism and excitement.

With the end of summer approaching, the Storm family was ready to embrace the next chapter of their lives. They had made significant strides in their personal and community projects, and they were eager to continue their journey of growth and discovery. As the days grew shorter and the first hints of fall appeared on the horizon, the Storm family prepared to transition into a new season, carrying with them the experiences and achievements of a vibrant and fulfilling summer.

AS THE FIRST HINTS of September began to cool the summer air, Riverbend and the Storm family prepared for the transition into fall. The end of summer was a time of reflection and planning for the future, and each member of the Storm family was busy wrapping up their summer projects and setting their sights on new goals.

Chloe's community mural project had been a tremendous success, and the mural had become a beloved part of Riverbend's landscape. The feedback from the community was overwhelmingly positive, and Chloe was proud of the way the project had brought people together. She was now focused on the next steps for the arts council, which included organizing a series of community art classes and workshops for the fall. These classes were designed to provide ongoing support for local artists and offer creative opportunities for residents of all ages.

With the summer's successes behind her, Chloe spent time planning the curriculum for the upcoming classes and reaching out to potential instructors. She was excited about the opportunity to continue fostering creativity in Riverbend and was eager to see how the community would respond to the new offerings.

Lucas wrapped up the summer farmers' market with a final event that celebrated the season's bounty. The market had been a resounding success, and Lucas was pleased with the community's engagement and the positive impact of the educational workshops. As the summer drew to a close, he focused on preparing the greenhouse for the upcoming fall season. He was planning to introduce a new line of seasonal produce and expand the greenhouse's offerings to include fall vegetables and herbs.

Lucas also started working on a new community initiative—a series of workshops on food preservation and cooking with seasonal ingredients. He hoped these workshops would help residents make the most of the fall harvest and promote sustainable living practices. The workshops would be held in the greenhouse and were designed to be both educational and interactive.

Jaxon returned to Riverbend with a renewed sense of purpose after his art residency. The experience had been transformative, and he was eager to apply what he had learned to his future projects. He was busy organizing a new exhibition to showcase the work he had created during the residency. The exhibition would be held at a local gallery and was intended to highlight the innovative techniques and themes he had explored.

Jaxon also planned to offer art workshops for local youth as part of his commitment to giving back to the community. These workshops would focus on various art techniques and encourage young artists to explore their creativity. Jaxon was excited about the opportunity to inspire and mentor the next generation of artists in Riverbend.

As September approached, the Storm family took time to prepare for the change in seasons. They enjoyed the last of the warm weather with outdoor activities and family outings. One weekend, they took a trip to a nearby nature reserve, exploring hiking trails and enjoying a picnic by the lake. It was a chance to relax and reconnect before the busyness of fall set in.

On a crisp September evening, the family gathered in the backyard for a barbecue. The air was cool and the sky was clear, offering a beautiful backdrop for their meal. Chloe, Lucas, and Jaxon shared their plans for the fall, discussing their upcoming projects and goals.

"We've had an amazing summer," Chloe said, her voice filled with satisfaction. "I'm excited about the new art classes and workshops. It feels great to see our community so engaged and inspired."

Lucas nodded in agreement. "The farmers' market was a highlight, and I'm looking forward to the fall workshops. I think they'll be a great addition to our community's efforts toward sustainability."

Jaxon smiled, feeling a sense of accomplishment. "The residency was a game-changer for me. I can't wait to share my new work and work with the kids in the art workshops. I think it's going to be a rewarding experience."

Lila looked around at her children, her heart full of pride. "I'm so proud of everything you've accomplished. It's been a season of growth and success. As we move into fall, I'm excited to see how we all continue to grow and contribute to our community."

As they finished their meal and enjoyed the cool evening breeze, the Storm family felt a deep sense of gratitude and anticipation. The summer had been a time of achievement and connection, and they were ready to embrace the new opportunities and challenges that fall would bring.

With the days growing shorter and the leaves beginning to change, the Storm family prepared for the transition into the new season. They looked forward to continuing their work, supporting each other's goals, and making a positive impact in Riverbend. As the first signs of autumn appeared, they felt a renewed sense of purpose and excitement for the future.

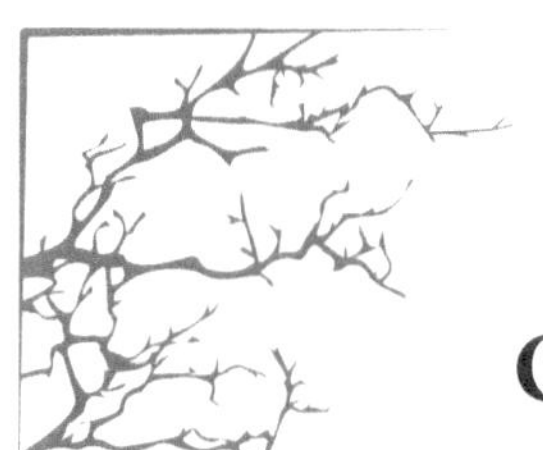

Chapter 10: Autumn Reflections

September ushered in a period of transition and reflection for Riverbend and the Storm family. The arrival of autumn brought cooler temperatures, vibrant foliage, and a renewed sense of focus as each member embarked on new projects and goals.

Chloe was deeply immersed in organizing the upcoming fall art classes and workshops. She had successfully secured a space at the community center for the classes and had begun reaching out to local artists and instructors to lead the sessions. The response had been enthusiastic, and Chloe was excited about the diverse range of classes that would be offered, from painting and sculpture to photography and digital arts.

To kick off the fall program, Chloe organized an open house event at the community center. The event would allow residents to learn more about the classes, meet the instructors, and sign up for sessions. Chloe hoped it would foster a sense of community and encourage participation in the arts.

Lucas's greenhouse was buzzing with activity as he prepared for the fall harvest. The transition from summer to fall brought changes to the greenhouse, with new crops being planted and seasonal produce becoming available. Lucas worked diligently to ensure that everything was in order for the upcoming harvest and the launch of his food preservation workshops.

The workshops were designed to teach residents how to preserve seasonal produce through techniques such as canning, freezing, and drying. Lucas was excited about the opportunity to share his knowledge and help others make the most of the fall harvest. He also planned to host cooking demonstrations that featured recipes using the preserved foods, making the workshops both educational and practical.

Jaxon's art exhibition, showcasing the work he created during his residency, was set to open at the local gallery. He had been busy preparing for the exhibition, including framing his pieces, designing promotional materials, and organizing the opening reception. The exhibition was a chance for Jaxon to share his artistic journey with the community and engage with art enthusiasts.

In addition to the exhibition, Jaxon was looking forward to starting his art workshops for local youth. He had designed the workshops to be engaging and inspiring, aiming to encourage young artists to explore their creativity and develop their skills. Jaxon was eager to see how the kids would respond to the new opportunities and hoped to make a positive impact on their artistic growth.

As September progressed, the Storm family found themselves wrapped in the rhythms of fall. The crisp air and changing leaves provided a picturesque backdrop for their activities, and they took time to enjoy the season's beauty. They participated in local fall festivals, visited apple orchards, and took scenic drives to appreciate the vibrant autumn colors.

One Saturday afternoon, the Storm family gathered for a picnic in the park to celebrate the beginning of fall. They enjoyed the cool breeze and the crunch of leaves underfoot as they shared a meal and reflected on their recent achievements.

Chloe discussed the upcoming open house and her excitement about the art classes. "I'm really looking forward to seeing how the community responds to the new program. It feels like a great way to continue building on the success of the mural project."

Lucas shared his enthusiasm for the food preservation workshops. "The response to the farmers' market has been so positive, and I think the workshops will be a great way to build on that momentum. I'm excited to help people learn new skills and make the most of the fall harvest."

Jaxon spoke about his exhibition and the art workshops. "The residency was an incredible experience, and I'm eager to share my new work with everyone. The workshops for the kids are something I'm especially excited about. I hope they find inspiration and joy in their creativity."

Lila, listening with pride, reflected on the family's accomplishments. "It's wonderful to see how each of you is contributing to our community in such meaningful ways. As we move into fall, I'm grateful for the opportunities we have and the positive impact we're making."

As the days grew shorter and the first signs of winter began to appear, the Storm family continued to embrace the season with optimism and enthusiasm. The fall programs and projects were well underway, and the family was eager to see the results of their hard work.

Chloe's art classes were a hit, with residents of all ages participating and exploring their creativity. The community mural had become a centerpiece of local pride, and the new classes were helping to foster a vibrant arts scene in Riverbend.

Lucas's food preservation workshops were well-attended, and participants appreciated the practical skills they were gaining. The cooking demonstrations were a highlight, offering delicious recipes and practical tips for making the most of the fall harvest.

Jaxon's art exhibition was a success, drawing positive reviews from both critics and the community. The art workshops for local youth were also well-received, with many young artists finding inspiration and encouragement from Jaxon's guidance.

As autumn settled in, the Storm family continued to support each other and celebrate their achievements. The season had been a time of growth, reflection, and new beginnings. They looked forward to the future with excitement and anticipation, ready to embrace the next chapter of their journey and the opportunities that lay ahead.

AS OCTOBER ROLLED IN, Riverbend was bathed in a golden hue from the changing leaves, and the crisp autumn air was filled with the scents of pumpkin spice and apple cider. The Storm family settled into their fall routines, each member deeply engaged in their projects and activities.

Chloe's art classes were thriving, and the community center buzzed with creative energy. The workshops had attracted a diverse group of participants, from seasoned artists seeking new inspiration to beginners eager to explore their artistic talents. Chloe took great satisfaction in seeing the students' progress and the sense of community that the classes fostered.

One evening, Chloe hosted a gallery night at the community center to showcase some of the work produced in the classes. The event was well-attended, with participants displaying their art and sharing their experiences with friends and family. The gallery night was a success, not only highlighting the talents of local artists but also strengthening the sense of artistic community in Riverbend.

Lucas's food preservation workshops were proving to be both educational and enjoyable. Participants were eager to learn about canning, freezing, and drying techniques, and the cooking demonstrations were particularly popular. Lucas enjoyed sharing his knowledge and seeing the positive reactions from the attendees.

To celebrate the success of the workshops, Lucas organized a Harvest Festival at the greenhouse. The festival featured local produce, homemade preserves, and cooking demonstrations. It was a festive event that brought together the community and showcased the fruits of Lucas's labor. The festival also included a pumpkin carving contest and a bake-off, adding a fun and competitive element to the day.

Jaxon's art exhibition had garnered significant attention, and his work was receiving acclaim from both local and regional art critics. The exhibition's success was a testament to his growth and creativity during his residency. Jaxon continued to engage with the community through his art workshops for youth, which were met with enthusiasm and excitement.

The workshops provided young artists with the opportunity to experiment with different techniques and develop their skills. Jaxon found it rewarding to see the kids' enthusiasm and creativity. He organized a final showcase for the youth participants, allowing them to display their work and celebrate their achievements.

As the days grew shorter and the weather became cooler, the Storm family took advantage of the season's offerings. They enjoyed local harvests, participated in fall festivals, and embraced the cozy, reflective atmosphere that autumn brings. They made it a point to spend quality time together, strengthening their bond and appreciating each other's achievements.

One chilly October evening, the family gathered around the fireplace for a cozy family dinner. They reflected on their recent experiences and discussed their plans for the coming months.

Chloe spoke about her satisfaction with the art classes and the impact they had on the community. "I'm thrilled with how the classes have turned out. It's been amazing to see the creativity and passion of the participants. I'm looking forward to continuing this momentum into the winter."

Lucas shared his thoughts on the Harvest Festival and the success of the food preservation workshops. "The festival was a great way to celebrate the fall season and the work we've done this year. The workshops have been rewarding, and I'm excited to see how we can continue to support sustainable practices."

Jaxon reflected on his exhibition and the youth workshops. "The residency was an incredible opportunity, and the response to my work has been more than I could have hoped for. The youth workshops have been a highlight for me. I'm looking forward to exploring new projects and continuing to engage with the community."

Lila listened with pride, grateful for the achievements and experiences of her children. "It's been a season of growth and fulfillment. Each of you has made such a positive impact in your own way. I'm proud of everything you've accomplished and excited to see where your passions will take you next."

As the evening wore on, the family enjoyed a hearty meal and the warmth of their togetherness. The autumn air outside was cool, but inside, the Storm family felt a deep sense of contentment and unity. They had embraced the season's opportunities and challenges with grace and enthusiasm, and they were ready to continue their journey into the coming months.

With the promise of winter on the horizon, the Storm family looked forward to the new experiences and opportunities that awaited them. They were excited to continue building on their successes and supporting each other as they ventured into the next chapter of their lives. As autumn leaves fell gently outside, the Storm family felt a renewed sense of purpose and anticipation for the future.

THE ARRIVAL OF NOVEMBER brought a crispness to the air that hinted at the approaching winter. Riverbend was preparing for the holiday season, and the Storm family was busy with their end-of-year projects and activities.

Chloe's art classes were in full swing, and she had organized a special fall art show at the community center. This event was intended to highlight the work of her students and celebrate the creativity fostered in her workshops. The gallery was adorned with colorful paintings, intricate sculptures, and mixed media pieces, each reflecting the individual style and growth of the artists.

The evening of the fall art show was bustling with excitement. Local residents, friends, and family gathered to admire the artwork and support the community's emerging artists. Chloe felt a deep sense of pride as she walked through the gallery, observing the attendees' admiration and engagement with the students' work.

Lucas's food preservation workshops had wrapped up, but his impact was still felt throughout the community. The Harvest Festival had been a tremendous success, and the recipes and preservation techniques shared during the workshops were being put to good use by local families. Lucas continued to support the community by providing tips and advice through a local newsletter dedicated to sustainable living and seasonal cooking.

As the weather grew colder, Lucas began preparing for winter gardening. He planned to introduce new greenhouse techniques to extend the growing season and explore new crop varieties suited to cooler temperatures. His commitment to sustainable agriculture remained strong, and he was excited to share his findings with the community.

Jaxon's art exhibition had concluded, and he was now focused on his ongoing youth art workshops. The final showcase for the young artists was a heartwarming event, with each participant proudly displaying their creations. The workshops had been a source of inspiration for many of the children, and Jaxon was thrilled with the progress they had made.

With the end of the year approaching, Jaxon started planning his next project. He was considering creating a new series of artworks inspired by the changing seasons and the themes of transformation and renewal. The idea excited him, and he looked forward to exploring new creative directions in the coming year.

As November progressed, the Storm family came together to celebrate Thanksgiving. They hosted a festive dinner at their home, inviting friends and neighbors to join in the holiday cheer. The table was filled with traditional dishes, and the warmth of the gathering provided a welcome contrast to the chilly weather outside.

During dinner, the family took a moment to express their gratitude for the past year's successes and support. Chloe shared her appreciation for the growth of the art classes and the positive feedback from the community. Lucas reflected on the success of the Harvest Festival and the impact of his workshops. Jaxon spoke about the inspiration he had gained from his residency and the joy of working with young artists.

Lila, with a heart full of pride, looked around at her family and their guests. "This year has been remarkable in so many ways. Each of you has accomplished so much, and I'm grateful for the support and love we share as a family. Here's to continued success and new adventures in the coming year."

The evening was filled with laughter, storytelling, and the joy of togetherness. The Storm family cherished these moments of connection and reflection, knowing that their collective efforts had made a meaningful difference in their lives and their community.

As the holiday season approached, the Storm family prepared for the winter months. They embraced the changing season with a sense of anticipation and readiness for the new opportunities that lay ahead. The year had been one of growth, achievement, and renewal, and they looked forward to continuing their journey with enthusiasm and determination.

With the first snowflakes beginning to fall, the Storm family settled into their winter routine. They enjoyed the cozy warmth of their home, celebrated the holidays with joy, and looked ahead to the new year with hope and excitement. The autumn had been a time of reflection and accomplishment, and as winter began, the Storm family was ready to embrace the future and continue making a positive impact in their community.

Chapter 11: One Book Closed: Ready to Start a New Story

As December arrived, Riverbend transformed into a winter wonderland. The first snowfall had coated the town in a layer of white, and the festive lights strung along the streets created a magical atmosphere. The Storm family, having wrapped up a year of notable achievements, took time to reflect on their journey and prepare for the new chapter ahead.

Chloe, Lucas, and Jaxon each spent the final weeks of the year reviewing their accomplishments and setting goals for the future. The art classes and workshops had been a tremendous success, and Chloe was already planning new projects for the coming year, including potential collaborations with local artists and expanded art education programs.

Lucas continued to explore innovative gardening techniques and planned to introduce new features to the greenhouse, such as hydroponics and winter crops. He was enthusiastic about sharing his knowledge with the community and was excited to see how the new projects would unfold.

Jaxon, inspired by his recent experiences, began sketching ideas for a new series of artworks that would reflect the themes of renewal and transformation. He was eager to experiment with new techniques and materials, and he envisioned his work contributing to a larger project that would engage and inspire the community.

The Storm family gathered for their annual end-of-year reflection, a tradition that allowed them to appreciate their successes and discuss their aspirations for the future. They met at a cozy local café, where they shared a meal and reminisced about the past year.

Chloe was the first to speak. "This year has been incredible. The art classes and community projects have been so fulfilling. I'm excited about the new ideas we have for the coming year and the potential for growth and creativity."

Lucas nodded, sipping his hot cocoa. "The Harvest Festival and the food preservation workshops were highlights for me. I'm looking forward to exploring new gardening techniques and continuing to support sustainable living in Riverbend."

Jaxon, with a thoughtful expression, added, "The art residency and the youth workshops were transformative experiences. I'm eager to dive into my new projects and see where my creativity takes me. I think we all have exciting opportunities ahead."

Lila, always the heart of the family, listened with a smile. "I'm so proud of everything each of you has accomplished. It's been a year of growth and connection, and I'm grateful for the love and support we share as a family. Here's to closing this chapter with pride and looking forward to the new adventures that await us."

As the conversation turned to their hopes and dreams for the new year, the Storm family felt a sense of excitement and anticipation. They were ready to embrace the opportunities that the coming year would bring, each with their own plans and aspirations.

With the holidays approaching, the family enjoyed festive activities, including decorating their home, attending local holiday events, and spending quality time together. The season was a time of joy and celebration, marking the end of a successful year and the beginning of a new journey.

On New Year's Eve, the Storm family gathered to celebrate the arrival of the new year. They reflected on their achievements and shared their resolutions and goals for the months ahead. The evening was filled with laughter, warmth, and the promise of new beginnings.

As the clock struck midnight, the Storm family raised their glasses in a toast to the new year. "To new adventures," Chloe said, her eyes sparkling with excitement. "To growth, creativity, and making a difference in our community."

"To family," Lucas added, "and to the strength and support we give each other."

"To new beginnings," Jaxon concluded, "and to the stories yet to be written."

The family clinked their glasses and embraced, ready to start the new year with optimism and determination. The past year had been one of significant achievements and personal growth, and as they looked forward to the future, they were eager to continue their journey together.

With the new year dawning, the Storm family closed one book and opened another, ready to write new stories and embrace the opportunities that lay ahead. The future was full of promise, and they were excited to face it with the same passion and dedication that had defined their past year.

THE FIRST DAYS OF JANUARY were marked by a sense of fresh beginnings and the lingering glow of the holiday season. The Storm family embraced the new year with a renewed sense of purpose and excitement. They each began to implement their plans, turning their resolutions into tangible actions.

Chloe, invigorated by the success of her art classes, began outlining her next big project: a collaborative community mural that would involve residents of all ages. She envisioned the mural as a celebration of Riverbend's diversity and creativity, and she started reaching out to local schools, community groups, and artists to contribute to the project. Chloe also planned a series of workshops leading up to the mural's creation, aimed at involving as many people as possible and fostering a sense of community involvement.

Lucas dove into his new gardening techniques with enthusiasm. He set up a section of the greenhouse for hydroponics and began experimenting with different crops suited for winter growth. His goal was to expand the greenhouse's capabilities and share the benefits of these innovative techniques with the community. He scheduled workshops to teach residents about hydroponics and winter gardening, hoping to inspire others to try their hand at sustainable agriculture.

Jaxon dedicated his time to developing his new series of artworks, which he planned to unveil in an upcoming gallery exhibition. He experimented with mixed media and unconventional materials, inspired by the themes of renewal and transformation. His work reflected his journey and the experiences of the past year, and he was excited to see how it would be received by the community.

The Storm family's commitment to their individual projects was complemented by their continued support for each other. They made it a point to come together regularly, sharing updates on their progress and offering encouragement. Their bond remained strong, and their shared experiences had deepened their appreciation for each other's achievements and aspirations.

One chilly January afternoon, the Storm family gathered at Chloe's studio to discuss the upcoming community mural project. Chloe had set up a preliminary design on a large canvas, and she was eager to share her vision.

"I'm really excited about this mural," Chloe said, her eyes shining with enthusiasm. "I think it's going to be a fantastic way to bring people together and celebrate our community's creativity. I've already started reaching out to local schools and community groups to get their input and involvement."

Lucas looked over the design, nodding in approval. "It's going to be amazing. I'm looking forward to seeing how it all comes together. And I'm excited to help with the workshops leading up to the mural's creation."

Jaxon, who had been working on his new art series, added, "The mural project sounds incredible. I'd love to be involved and contribute some of my own work or ideas. It's great to see how we're all finding ways to connect with and inspire the community."

Lila, always supportive, smiled at her children. "It's wonderful to see each of you so passionate about your projects. I'm proud of how you're continuing to make a difference in Riverbend. This mural will be a testament to the creativity and spirit of our community."

As the conversation continued, the family brainstormed ideas for the mural's themes and design elements. They discussed incorporating symbols and images that represented Riverbend's unique character and the diverse experiences of its residents. Chloe planned to host a series of community meetings to gather input and ideas from local residents, ensuring that the mural would truly reflect the collective spirit of the town.

With their plans taking shape, the Storm family embraced the new year with optimism and determination. Each member was excited about their individual projects and the impact they hoped to make in their community. They were ready to face the challenges and opportunities that lay ahead, knowing that their shared commitment to growth and creativity would guide them.

As January drew to a close, the Storm family continued to work on their respective projects, each finding fulfillment and joy in their pursuits. They celebrated their progress with regular family dinners, where they shared their successes and discussed their future goals.

The new year had begun with promise and excitement, and the Storm family was eager to continue their journey. They closed the chapter on a successful year with gratitude and anticipation, ready to start writing new stories and making a positive impact in Riverbend. With each new day, they embraced the possibilities of the future and the opportunities that awaited them.

FEBRUARY ARRIVED WITH a hint of warmth in the air, signaling the end of winter and the promise of spring. The Storm family continued to make strides in their respective projects, and the excitement about their new ventures was palpable.

Chloe's community mural project was in full swing. The initial workshops had been a success, with residents of all ages eagerly participating. Chloe had organized a series of meetings to gather ideas and feedback, and she was thrilled with the creative contributions from the community. The mural was taking shape, featuring vibrant colors and images that represented the town's spirit and diversity. Chloe also started planning a series of public events leading up to the mural's completion, including artist talks and interactive sessions where residents could contribute directly to the painting process.

Lucas's hydroponics experiments in the greenhouse were showing promising results. He had successfully grown several crops using the new techniques and was preparing to showcase the benefits of hydroponics in his upcoming workshops. Lucas was excited to share his findings with the community and was optimistic about the potential for year-round gardening in Riverbend. He also began working on a guide to help residents start their own hydroponic systems at home, aiming to promote sustainable agriculture and self-sufficiency.

Jaxon's new art series was coming together beautifully. He had completed several pieces that captured the themes of renewal and transformation, and he was preparing for an exhibition at the local gallery. The series was receiving positive feedback from early previews, and Jaxon was excited to share his work with a broader audience. He also planned to incorporate some interactive elements into the exhibition, allowing visitors to engage with the art in new and meaningful ways.

The Storm family's collective efforts were beginning to bear fruit, and they continued to support each other as they pursued their goals. Their shared commitment to their projects and to each other strengthened their bond and provided a sense of unity and purpose.

One evening, as the family gathered for dinner, Chloe shared the latest updates on the mural project. "The mural is really coming together. We've had so many people contribute their ideas, and it's incredible to see it all come to life. I'm especially excited about the upcoming events where we'll have more opportunities for community involvement."

Lucas, who had been preparing for his hydroponics workshops, chimed in. "I'm looking forward to the workshops. I think people will be really interested in learning about hydroponics and how it can help with year-round gardening. I'm also excited about sharing the guide I've been working on."

Jaxon, reflecting on his art series, said, "The exhibition is almost ready, and I'm thrilled with how the pieces have turned out. I think the interactive elements will make the experience even more engaging for visitors. I'm looking forward to seeing how people connect with the work."

Lila, ever supportive, smiled at her children. "It's amazing to see how each of you is contributing to our community in such meaningful ways. The mural, the hydroponics workshops, and the art exhibition all reflect your passions and talents. I'm so proud of everything you're accomplishing."

As February continued, the Storm family continued to make progress on their projects and prepare for their upcoming events. The sense of anticipation and excitement was palpable, and they eagerly looked forward to the opportunities that the coming months would bring.

With spring just around the corner, the family began to make plans for the future. Chloe envisioned expanding her art programs and exploring new community art initiatives. Lucas was excited about the potential for hydroponics to revolutionize local gardening practices. Jaxon was already brainstorming ideas for his next series of artworks and potential collaborations.

The Storm family approached the new year with optimism and a sense of possibility. They had closed one chapter with success and were ready to start a new story filled with opportunities for growth and creativity. As they embraced the changing seasons and the promise of new beginnings, they remained committed to making a positive impact in their community and supporting each other every step of the way. Chapter 11: One Book Closed: Ready to Start a New Story (Continued)

February arrived with a hint of warmth in the air, signaling the end of winter and the promise of spring. The Storm family continued to make strides in their respective projects, and the excitement about their new ventures was palpable.

Chloe's community mural project was in full swing. The initial workshops had been a success, with residents of all ages eagerly participating. Chloe had organized a series of meetings to gather ideas and feedback, and she was thrilled with the creative contributions from the community. The mural was taking shape, featuring vibrant colors and images that represented the town's spirit and diversity. Chloe also started planning a series of public events leading up to the mural's completion, including artist talks and interactive sessions where residents could contribute directly to the painting process.

Lucas's hydroponics experiments in the greenhouse were showing promising results. He had successfully grown several crops using the new techniques and was preparing to showcase the benefits of hydroponics in his upcoming workshops. Lucas was excited to share his findings with the community and was optimistic about the potential for year-round gardening in Riverbend. He also began working on a guide to help residents start their own hydroponic systems at home, aiming to promote sustainable agriculture and self-sufficiency.

Jaxon's new art series was coming together beautifully. He had completed several pieces that captured the themes of renewal and transformation, and he was preparing for an exhibition at the local gallery. The series was receiving positive feedback from early previews, and Jaxon was excited to share his work with a broader audience. He also planned to incorporate some interactive elements into the exhibition, allowing visitors to engage with the art in new and meaningful ways.

The Storm family's collective efforts were beginning to bear fruit, and they continued to support each other as they pursued their goals. Their shared commitment to their projects and to each other strengthened their bond and provided a sense of unity and purpose.

One evening, as the family gathered for dinner, Chloe shared the latest updates on the mural project. "The mural is really coming together. We've had so many people contribute their ideas, and it's incredible to see it all come to life. I'm especially excited about the upcoming events where we'll have more opportunities for community involvement."

Lucas, who had been preparing for his hydroponics workshops, chimed in. "I'm looking forward to the workshops. I think people will be really interested in learning about hydroponics and how it can help with year-round gardening. I'm also excited about sharing the guide I've been working on."

Jaxon, reflecting on his art series, said, "The exhibition is almost ready, and I'm thrilled with how the pieces have turned out. I think the interactive elements will make the experience even more engaging for visitors. I'm looking forward to seeing how people connect with the work."

Lila, ever supportive, smiled at her children. "It's amazing to see how each of you is contributing to our community in such meaningful ways. The mural, the hydroponics workshops, and the art exhibition all reflect your passions and talents. I'm so proud of everything you're accomplishing."

As February continued, the Storm family continued to make progress on their projects and prepare for their upcoming events. The sense of anticipation and excitement was palpable, and they eagerly looked forward to the opportunities that the coming months would bring.

With spring just around the corner, the family began to make plans for the future. Chloe envisioned expanding her art programs and exploring new community art initiatives. Lucas was excited about the potential for hydroponics to revolutionize local gardening practices. Jaxon was already brainstorming ideas for his next series of artworks and potential collaborations.

The Storm family approached the new year with optimism and a sense of possibility. They had closed one chapter with success and were ready to start a new story filled with opportunities for growth and creativity. As they embraced the changing seasons and the promise of new beginnings, they remained committed to making a positive impact in their community and supporting each other every step of the way.

Epilogue: New Beginnings

As spring blossomed in Riverbend, the town came alive with vibrant colors and renewed energy. The Storm family, having navigated a year of significant change and growth, was eager to embrace the new season and the opportunities it brought.

Chloe's community mural project had reached its final stages. The mural, a magnificent tapestry of colors and symbols representing Riverbend's spirit, was unveiled in a grand celebration. The event drew a large crowd, and the joy and pride in the community were palpable. Chloe looked on with satisfaction as residents admired the mural, marveling at the collective effort that had brought it to life. The mural became a beloved landmark in Riverbend, a testament to the power of community and creativity.

Lucas's hydroponics workshops had been a resounding success. The greenhouse was flourishing with new crops, and residents were enthusiastic about the potential for year-round gardening. Lucas's guide on hydroponics had been well-received, and he continued to support the community with tips and advice. His efforts were making a tangible difference, and he was excited to explore further innovations in sustainable agriculture.

Jaxon's art exhibition had been a highlight of the local art scene. His new series, exploring themes of renewal and transformation, was met with acclaim from both critics and visitors. The interactive elements of the exhibition had engaged audiences in meaningful ways, and Jaxon was already planning his next project. His work continued to inspire and connect with people, reflecting his growth and creative journey.

The Storm family enjoyed the warmth of spring as they celebrated their individual and collective achievements. They spent time together outdoors, appreciating the beauty of the season and the fulfillment of their accomplishments. Family dinners, walks through blooming parks, and shared laughter became cherished moments of connection and joy.

As the year progressed, the Storm family remained focused on their goals and continued to support each other. They looked forward to new projects and opportunities, confident in their ability to make a positive impact in their community. Their dedication to their passions and their commitment to each other had become the foundation of their success.

Reflecting on the past year, Lila felt a deep sense of pride and gratitude. The journey had been marked by challenges and triumphs, and the Storm family had emerged stronger and more united. They had closed one chapter with grace and had embraced the promise of new beginnings with enthusiasm.

As the sun set on a beautiful spring day, the Storm family gathered for a quiet moment of reflection. They acknowledged the progress they had made and the growth they had experienced, both individually and together. Their journey had been one of discovery and achievement, and they were ready to continue writing their story with hope and determination.

The future was bright with possibilities, and the Storm family faced it with confidence and excitement. They knew that, with their shared commitment and unwavering support, they could tackle any challenge and seize every opportunity that came their way. As they looked forward to the next chapter of their lives, they did so with a sense of anticipation and a heart full of hope.

In the ever-changing tapestry of life, the Storm family had found their place, creating a legacy of creativity, resilience, and love. And as they stepped into the future, they carried with them the lessons learned and the dreams nurtured, ready to embrace whatever came next.

SUMMER IN RIVERBEND was a time of vibrant activity and celebration. The Storm family, having navigated a year of profound changes and accomplishments, embraced the season with joy and a renewed sense of purpose.

Chloe's community mural had become a central fixture in Riverbend, sparking ongoing conversations and fostering a sense of pride among the residents. Inspired by the mural's success, Chloe initiated a series of public art events and workshops. These events included collaborative art projects, street fairs, and pop-up galleries, all aimed at continuing to engage the community in creative endeavors. Her efforts contributed to a growing appreciation for the arts in Riverbend, and she was delighted to see how her passion had inspired others.

Lucas's work with hydroponics had led to a significant shift in local gardening practices. The techniques he had introduced were being adopted by households across Riverbend, and the greenhouse had become a hub of activity and innovation. Lucas partnered with local schools to incorporate sustainable gardening into their curricula, teaching students about the benefits of hydroponics and fostering a new generation of environmentally conscious gardeners. The success of his workshops and the growing interest in sustainable living were gratifying, and he looked forward to exploring new ways to enhance local agriculture.

Jaxon's art continued to make waves, and his latest project—a series of collaborative pieces involving local artists and community members—was gaining attention. The project aimed to capture the collective spirit of Riverbend through art, and Jaxon was thrilled to see how his vision was coming to life. The pieces were displayed in various public spaces, each telling a unique story and inviting viewers to reflect on their own experiences and connections to the community.

As summer drew to a close, the Storm family took time to enjoy the fruits of their labor. They traveled together on a family vacation, exploring new places and making memories. The trip was a chance for them to relax, reconnect, and celebrate their achievements. They reflected on their journey, sharing stories and dreams for the future as they enjoyed each other's company.

Back in Riverbend, life continued to thrive with the changes the Storm family had contributed to. The community was vibrant and engaged, and the impact of the mural, the hydroponics workshops, and the art projects was evident in the renewed enthusiasm and collaborative spirit among residents.

As autumn approached, the Storm family returned to their routines with fresh energy and excitement for the upcoming season. Chloe was preparing for new art initiatives and exhibitions, Lucas was developing additional sustainable projects, and Jaxon was planning new creative endeavors. Each member of the family was eager to build on their successes and continue making a positive impact in their community.

Lila, reflecting on the past year, felt a profound sense of fulfillment. The journey had been one of growth, transformation, and connection. She was proud of her children's achievements and the ways in which they had embraced their passions and contributed to Riverbend's vibrant community. As the family gathered for a celebratory dinner, Lila took a moment to express her gratitude and share her hopes for the future.

"Looking back on this year, I'm filled with pride and joy," Lila said. "Each of you has made such a difference in our community, and it's been incredible to watch you pursue your passions with such dedication. As we move forward, let's continue to support each other and embrace the opportunities that come our way. The future is bright, and I'm excited to see where our journey takes us next."

With the promise of new beginnings and the strength of their shared experiences, the Storm family looked forward to the next chapter of their lives. They were ready to face the future with optimism and determination, confident in their ability to create positive change and continue their journey of growth and discovery.

As the seasons changed and new stories unfolded, the Storm family remained a beacon of creativity, resilience, and love, ready to embrace whatever came next with hope and enthusiasm.

Thank You for Reading

Thank you for taking the time to read this book. Your support means the world to me, and I am deeply grateful for your interest and enthusiasm. I hope you enjoyed the journey and found the story as engaging and meaningful as I intended it to be.

If you enjoyed this book, please consider leaving a review or sharing your thoughts with others. Your feedback helps support and encourage authors, and it is greatly appreciated.

Thank you once again for your support and for being a part of this literary adventure.

Don't miss out!

Visit the website below and you can sign up to receive emails whenever Ms.Sue publishes a new book. There's no charge and no obligation.

https://books2read.com/r/B-A-VKJGC-PJBYE

BOOKS 2 READ

Connecting independent readers to independent writers.

www.ingramcontent.com/pod-product-compliance
Lightning Source LLC
Chambersburg PA
CBHW051218160726
47994CB00002B/650